A COMPILATION OF MEALS,
MOMENTS & MEMORIES

NANI'S COOKBOOK

Cherished family recipes
from her kitchen to yours.

Jessica Greenlow & Family

Nani's Cookbook: *Cherished family recipes from her kitchen to yours.* is a work of our own creation.

The information in this book was correct at the time of publication. The Authors do not assume any liability for loss or damage caused by errors or omissions. The stories & memories included within these pages are from our personal perspective & experiences & have been written as such.

Copyright © 2025 by Jessica Greenlow & Family

All rights reserved.

No part of this book may be reproduced or transmitted in any form or by any means, electronic or mechanical, including photocopying, recording, or by any information & retrieval systems, without the written permission of the Publisher, except where permitted by law.

ISBN - 978-1-961185-72-2

Professional Photos courtesy:
Shaunna Lockwood of Lockwood Photo & Film - *www.lockwoodphotoandfilm.com*
Sarah Tyrrell of SJT Photography - *www.sjtphotographynh.com*
Pat Robinson Photography - *www.patrobinsonphotography.com*

Cover Design, Book Formatting & Layout by megs thompson, megswrites llc
www.megswrites.com

www.inomniaparatuspublishing.com

TABLE OF CONTENTS

Mise En Place: *Before we begin...*   1

Introduction   7

Holiday Recipes   15

    Thanksgiving   17

    Popi's Birthday   33

    Holiday Treats   47

    Christmas Eve   79

    Christmas Morning   87

    Christmas Dinner   98

    St. Patrick's Day   111

    Mother's Day   119

    Father's Day   131

    Independence Day   139

    Nani's Birthday   149

Everyday Recipes	**159**
Nani's General Cooking Terms & Definitions	**227**
Supportive Sides & Serving Suggestions	**235**
Seasonal Fresh Vegetable & Fruit Buying Guide	**241**
Spice & Herb Seasoning Guide for New Cooks	**251**
Household Hints *(Or Hacks As You Kids Call Them)*	**259**
Cheese Guide: Common & Uncommon	**267**
Nani's Recipes for Life	**273**
Dear Nani: *A Letter To Our Beloved Matriarch*	**277**
To My Family: *A Note from Nani*	**285**
Full Index of Recipes	**289**

MISE EN PLACE

Before we begin...

Some moments in life exist outside of time, suspended in a space where love lingers, unshaken by the ticking of a clock. Time stands still & that's how it feels to be with my grandmother.

With Nani, time is never rushed. Instead, it stretches, softens, it reconfigures to make room for us. Whether I was curled up in her lap as a child, my tiny hands tracing the delicate lines of her own, or sitting beside her as an adult, sharing tea, stories & an unspoken understanding, the world has always felt a little slower, a little kinder, a little more wonderful, in her presence.

Nani has always dreamed of writing a cookbook. Not for the fame or recognition, but for us...for her family. She's imagined a simple collection of recipes, printed & bound together. Something she can pass down to her children & grandchildren as a keepsake of tradition; a tangible piece of the love she pours into every meal.

To me, though, the idea of a simple cookbook from Nani has never seemed like enough. Instead, I dreamed that Nani's Cookbook should be a grand creation to honor the hands that have prepared the dishes within its pages, the echoes of the voices that have filled her kitchen over countless holiday celebrations, the decades of laughter that have simmered & spilled from one room to another & the impression she leaves on the hearts of all who know her.

Nani, my mother DeeDee & I spent nights around her dinner table, pens in hand, scribbling down recipes, reminiscing about which dishes were each family member's favorite & which rendition we'd choose to pass on to future generations. We laughed as we debated over exact measurements. All three of us knowing full well that Nani has never measured anything. She doesn't need to. Somehow, she always just knows. No matter the recipe, the dish, or how long it's been since she made it last, Nani just knows every ingredient by feel, by intuition, by love. We made lists, we planned & then... as it so often does, life got in the way.

Four years slipped by before I even considered returning to the cookbook project. Between career building, raising babies, countless doctor appointments, & the relentless rhythm of daily life, the cookbook sat waiting, unfinished, gathering dust. Then, the summer of 2024 arrived & it was, to date, the hardest season our family had faced yet. Our beloved matriarch needed the support of her family more than ever. Hospital visits turned into quiet prayers, whispered in sterile rooms where time felt fragile & uncertain. Yet even in the heaviness, I felt a calling. I knew that I had to finish what we had started together.

Because this project needed to be more than a cookbook. This is Nani's legacy.

Sitting with Popi at their large dining room table, I asked for his blessing to proceed with this project, to honor Nani in the best way I knew how, by tapping into the things she loves most in life - faith, food & her family. I'll never forget that night, my mother & I, holding his hands, while the weight of things, of our current situation, settled into my heart. "*I need to do this,*" I told him. "*Not just for us, but for her. For everyone who has ever been nourished by Nani's love. She deserves more than a self-printed book on the coffee table. Nani deserves to see her story, her recipes, her legacy on shelves, in homes, in the hands of families around the world. Because the love she has given extends far beyond the walls of our family.*"

This journey, bringing Nani's dream to life—has been a tender dance between joy & longing. It's been a privilege, a labor of love, & a quiet ache all at once. I often think about the lifetime we've shared—the comfort of her arms, the calm in her voice, the steady presence she's always been. I find myself tucking away every moment each time I've called to ask how to fix a dish & hearing how her endearing response begins with, "*oh dear,*" every kitchen tip, every look that means so much more than words & how she has always known just what was needed both in & out of the kitchen. I've been holding on to the moments a little more closely knowing that one day, these memories will speak to me in quieter ways. I imagine her beside me in the garden, at the stove, or on the love seat—not just as a presence, but as a feeling, a whisper in my heart. And when the *'tea-for-two'* tradition becomes more memory than ritual, I'll still pour a cup for us.

I take solace in the knowledge that I will always have this.
We will always have this.

We will carry forward the lessons she's wrapped into every day: to do all things through love, to lead with a grateful heart & to meet the world with open arms, kindness & faith.

I will continue to carry her spirit with me, in the way I cook, in the way I nurture & in the way I love. *(Note to self: Always channel your inner Nani)*

My grandmother is my best friend, my confidante & one of my greatest teachers. Bringing her story to life has been an honor, a pleasure & a delight. Because everyone deserves to have a Nani, someone to guide them gently, to listen intently & to love them fiercely. For those who never had a Nani of their own, this book is our family's way of sharing her with you.

Because a love like Nani's, like the very best recipes, is meant to be passed on.

- Jessica 'Jessi' Rice Greenlow
(Creative Author, Granddaughter)

Mise en place, is a French term for the first step of every chef's process. It roughly translates to 'gathering of pieces' or 'everything in the right place' & ensures that the necessary tools & ingredients are where they should be for a successful baking or cooking experience.

INTRODUCTION

This book is a collection of timeless recipes, tested & perfected by our family's inspirational matriarch, Nani Judy.

Our large, gregarious family's story all started when a 14-year-old girl named Judy made a hurried call to the common room of the local army base & a young EOD (Explosive Ordnance Disposal) soldier named Gordon answered the line. The two strangers struck up a conversation & as the saying goes, the rest is history. According to Judy, she recalls asking her sister Barbara if it was possible to fall in love with a voice. When Gordon reflects back on that first conversation, he says that he was absolutely mesmerized by her voice & their easy conversation.

These phone dates continued until the Summer, when Judy went to the Cape with her family. Because they had no phone at the beach house, the two young lovebirds continued communicating by exchanging letters & when she returned home in August, they set a date for Gordon to visit her home. This would be the first time the two had ever met in person. When Judy's mother answered the door, she thought young Gordon was quite handsome, something she told her daughter later that afternoon. Judy's father wasn't a fan of his daughter's suitor though, simply because he was in the military. From that day on, there was no denying that the two were in love.

When Gordon recounts that first moment, when he stepped off the bus & saw her for the first time, he knew that no one else compared & he was meant to be with Judy. She was & still is his one true love.

Less than one year after that first phone call, Gordon & Judy asked her parents for their signature to receive court approval to be married. When it came time to speak before a judge, Judy's mother went on & on & on about what a great guy Gordon was, finally, the judge had to tell her to stop. After all, he wasn't concerned about how great Gordon was, he was concerned if Judy was ready to get married at the young age of 15. Needless to say, the court approved & on November 10th, 1962 at Saint Joseph's Church, the two were married, beginning what would become a lifetime of adventure, love, laughter, world travel, food, family & memories.

Wasting no time at all, the young couple welcomed 3 children within their first 3 years of marriage, all while traveling for Gordon's assignments with the United States Army. While the consistent travel made it difficult to settle into a community, Judy found solace in caring for her family, nurturing her children as they grew & taking special care of her husband, Gordon.

Moving did have its upsides, though. The family of 5 was able to visit & experience countless countries & cultures around the world, further inspiring Judy's love for exploring various cuisines & traditions; something she's instilled in her children, her grandchildren, her great-grandchildren & countless generations to come. One of Judy's favorite things to do was to spoil Gordon with different Norwegian dishes, a nod to his family's heritage, adding her own tweaks to merge them with her own family's Italian flavors.

Judith, Judy, Mom, Nani - She goes by many names, but no matter what you call her, she's served as the Matriarch of our family & will continue to do so for generations to come. Her belief that what matters most in life is to have your friends, family & loved ones around you, to share your bounties & express gratitude freely will continue to live on through the recipes she's given us to feed both the body & the soul.

Today, her children & grandchildren continue to rely on Nani's kitchen magic for help when choosing the perfect meal for their special occasions, figuring out

what spice is missing from a dish & of course, teaching their own children (her great-grandchildren) the importance of keeping the kitchen as the heart of a home.

Within these pages, we've set out to share some of our most cherished meals, moments, memories & everyday life lessons learned from & experienced with Nani. Because, as Nani has taught us, there is nothing in life that can't be fixed or improved with a good home-cooked meal & loved ones by your side.

We hope that by flipping through these pages, you & your family are inspired to find fun & enjoyment in the kitchen the way we have.

Our Family

- **Judith 'Judy' & Gordon Avron** — Nani & Popi
  - **Gordon 'Chip' & Kate Avron**
    - Chelsea & Rob Henggeler
      - Laura Leggiero
    - Michelle & James Heath
      - Alyssa (11)
        - Alana (8)
          - Anderson (4)
  - **Mark Avron & Kristine Costello-Avron**
    - Jake Costello
    - Collin & Ava Delia
      - Marlon (2)
    - Stephanie Avron & Sean Heeney
      - Paige (11)
        - Keegan (6)
  - **DeAnna 'DeeDee' & Chuck Rice**
    - Nicholas 'Nick' Rice & Carrisa Kotsopoulos
      - Hunter (4)
        - Antheia (2)
    - Jessica 'Jessi' & James Greenlow
      - Hayden (3)

OUR FAMILY BLESSINGS

Bless us, O Lord,
for these thy gifts,
which we are about to receive
from thy bounty,
through Christ our Lord.
Amen.

God is great. God is good.
Let us thank him for our food.
Amen.

Come lord Jesus, be our guest.
Let these gifts to us be blessed.
Amen.

HOLIDAY RECIPES

THANKSGIVING

Our family celebrates quite a few holidays throughout the year together & food is always at the heart of those gatherings. But there's something especially meaningful about Thanksgiving.

It's the time when most everyone makes an extra effort to return home—no matter where life has taken them—to gather around Nani & Popi's table once more. It's a day filled with familiar faces, shared stories & dishes seasoned with love & laughter.

So, it feels only fitting that our book begins here—with Thanksgiving, a celebration of togetherness, gratitude & the warmth of coming home.

OUR MENU

- Roasted Turkey & Gravy
- Grandma Avron's Prune Dressing
- Bread Dressing (Stuffing)
- Cranberry Relish
- Green Beans with Bacon
- Sweet Potatoes
- Mashed Potatoes
- Honey Garlic Glazed Carrots
- Pumpkin Pie
- Popi's Favorite Apple Pie

ROASTED TURKEY & GRAVY

Ingredients

Turkey:
whole turkey, *thawed*
butter
olive oil
homemade stuffing *(see recipe for Grandma's Avron's Prune Dressing or Bread Stuffing)*
16+ cups chicken, turkey, or vegetable stock
salt & pepper to taste

Gravy:
2 tbsp cornstarch
1 cup broth *(turkey or chicken)*
turkey gizzards, heart & broth, cooked)
roasted turkey pan drippings
¼-½ tsp poultry seasoning *(a few shakes as Nani says)*
salt & pepper to taste
½ cup heavy cream

Directions

Remove the bag containing the gizzards, heart, neck & liver from inside the bird. Dispose of the liver.

Place gizzards, heart & neck into a small pot, cover with water & a dash of poultry seasoning.

Simmer on medium heat until the meat on neck begins separating from the bone.

Remove neck from the pot either dispose or set aside to be eaten separately.

Transfer gizzards, heart & broth into another container to cool.

Cover & refrigerate until the turkey has been cooked & you're ready to prepare the gravy.

Preheat oven to 350 degrees & organize oven racks as needed to allow for turkey.

In a clean sink, rinse the turkey inside & out.

Pat dry & stuff turkey with homemade stuffing.

Truss the bird & generously rub with butter or olive oil.

Place turkey, breast side up, into the roasting bag, then into a large roasting pan.

Tie the roasting bag closed & using a knife, cut 3-4 slits into the top, to allow steam out while roasting.

Roast turkey according to the timetable/instructions that came with the bird.

When there's approx. 1 hour left of roasting-time, start checking the bird temperature. *The turkey is finished when an internal thermometer reads 160 degrees.*

Remove the turkey from the oven & carefully scoop the stuffing out, into a serving dish. Be sure to save the turkey drippings to make your gravy.

Optional: If you'd like to prepare your turkey in advance, allow it to cool then carve. Place the meat into a large shallow pan & cover with enough turkey broth to cover the meat. Cover the pan with foil & refrigerate. The next day, when ready to serve, place the pan into a preheated oven & warm until it reaches desired temperature. Move to a platter before serving.

To Make Gravy:

Pour broth from cooking turkey gizzards & heart into blender.

Add cornstarch & broth.

Blend well.

Carefully pour into a medium pot with roasted turkey pan drippings.

Add poultry season & heat to boil, stirring constantly to avoid lumps.

If your gravy is too thick, add more broth. If it's too thin, add a cornstarch slurry. (Mix approx. 1 tsp of cornstarch in 2 tsp of cold water in a small bowl, then add to the hot gravy & stir well. Make sure the gravy is boiling before adding cornstarch.)

Once your gravy is at the right consistency, add cream. Stir well.

Keep gravy hot until you're ready to serve.

Optional: If you have members of your family that enjoy Giblets in their gravy, you can roughly chop the cooked heart & gizzards, adding them to a portion of the cooked gravy.

Family is the Best Ingredient

Cooking is a communal activity. Family traditions, memories shared around the table & the togetherness of time spent in the kitchen are what make food truly special. Never forget that the people you share these experiences with are the most important part of any meal.
   -Nani

GRANDMA AVRON'S PRUNE DRESSING

Ingredients

2 apples, peeled & diced
1 cup of pitted prunes
½ cup of raisins
1 cup celery, diced
2 onions, chopped
1 bag seasoned stuffing mix *(not stove top)*
2 cups chicken or turkey stock or broth
1 stick of butter
poultry seasoning, salt & pepper to taste

Directions:

Preheat oven to 350 degrees.

Mix broth & butter in a large pot on the stove until butter is melted.

Add all other ingredients & mix well.

Pour into a buttered casserole dish, cover with aluminum foil & bake for 30-45 minutes.

Remove from oven & if your dressing appears dry, add a bit more broth or liquid from the turkey pan.

Serve hot & enjoy!

BREAD DRESSING
(Stuffing)

Ingredients

1 bag stuffing mix *(not stove top)*
2 onions, chopped
1 cup celery, diced
1 carton of chicken or turkey stock or broth
2 sticks of butter
poultry seasoning, salt & pepper to taste

Optional: chestnuts (cooked & mashed), mushrooms (diced), or a roll of ground sausage (cooked)

Directions:

On stove, in a large pot melt butter with onion & celery.

Cook for 5 minutes or so until veggies are translucent.

Add broth & remaining ingredients to pot.

Mix thoroughly & allow to cool.

Stuff both the cavity & neck area of your turkey with dressing, or put into a buttered casserole dish & cook alongside turkey in oven.

Hint: If you have cheese cloth handy, you can place the dressing in the cheese cloth & then stuff into the cavity of the bird. This makes it much easier to pull out.

Serve hot & enjoy!

CRANBERRY RELISH

Ingredients

1 bag of fresh cranberries
1 medium apple, cored & peeled
1 small orange, not peeled
1 cup sugar
½ tsp cinnamon
½ tsp ground cloves

Directions:

Place cranberries, apple & orange into a food processor.

Pulse until it reaches a relish consistency.

Pour into a medium bowl.

Add sugar, cinnamon & cloves.

Mix well.

Store in a sealed container & chill for at least 1 day before serving.

GREEN BEANS WITH BACON

Ingredients

1/2 lb bacon, chopped
1 small yellow onion, or large shallot, chopped
4 cloves garlic, pressed or minced
2 lbs fresh green beans, trimmed
1 tsp red pepper flakes
salt & pepper to taste

Directions:

Preheat oven to 425°F

In a skillet begin cooking bacon over medium heat, stirring occasionally.

After approx 5 minutes add onion, garlic & red pepper flakes to bacon. Stir well.

Continue cooking for another 5 minutes.

Place trimmed green beans in a large baking pan & top with bacon mixture. Mix well.

Bake for 10 minutes, carefully remove from oven & stir before baking for another 7-10 minutes.

SWEET POTATOES

Ingredients

4 sweet potatoes, either baked or boiled
1/4 cup butter
maple syrup or brown sugar
cinnamon
chopped pecans

Optional: mini marshmallows

Directions:

Preheat over to 350 degrees.

Remove the skin from potatoes.

Slice butter & spread over the top of potatoes.

Drizzle with maple syrup or brown sugar & a pinch of cinnamon.

Sprinkle with chopped pecans & bake for 20 minutes or until butter & sugar are melted.

Optional Topping: Once cooked, carefully remove from oven & top with a thin layer of mini marshmallows. Broil in oven just until melted & lightly toasted.

Patience is Key

The best meals take time. Whether it's letting dough rise or simmering a sauce for hours every Sunday, good things come with patience. Life doesn't always need to be rushed, sometimes the best moments unfold in their own time.

—Nani

MASHED POTATOES

Ingredients

5 pounds potatoes *(we prefer Yukon gold)*
6 tbsp butter
1 cup milk, room temperature
fresh chives, finely chopped
salt & pepper to taste
Optional: 4 oz cream cheese, room temperature

Directions:

Peel all potatoes & cut into evenly-sized pieces approx. 1 inch thick & place into a large stockpot full of cold water.

Cover & bring to a soft boil over medium-high heat.

After 30 minutes, test doneness with a fork. It should pierce the potato easily.

Carefully drain all water from the pot & set potatoes aside.

In a smaller saucepan melt butter over low heat.

Once melted, pour milk into the pan with butter & set aside.

Using your preferred method, mash potatoes to your desired consistency.

Pour melted butter & milk mixture into potatoes. Stir well.

If desired: Fold cream cheese into potato mixture.

Season to taste with salt & pepper. Top with chopped chives. Serve & enjoy with more butter or your favorite gravy.

HONEY GARLIC GLAZED CARROTS

Ingredients

2 lb carrots, peeled
1 ½ tbsp honey
2 garlic cloves, minced
3 tbsp butter, melted
½ lemon
salt & pepper to taste

Directions:

Preheat oven to 425 degrees.

Clean & cut carrots in half lengthwise, then slice on the diagonal into 2-inch lengths.

In a large bowl, mix honey, garlic & butter.

Add carrots & toss to coat evenly.

Spread evenly on a cookie or shallow baking sheet.

Roast in the oven for 15 minutes.

Carefully remove from oven & stir before roasting for another 10 minutes.

Sprinkle with juice from ½ lemon & enjoy.

PUMPKIN PIE

Ingredients

¾ cup sugar
½ tsp salt
1 tsp cinnamon
½ tsp ground ginger
¼ tsp ground cloves
¼ tsp nutmeg
2 eggs
1 can pumpkin puree
1 can evaporated milk
1 unbaked pie crust

Directions:

Preheat oven to 425 degrees.

In a small bowl combine sugar, salt, cinnamon, ginger, cloves & nutmeg. Set aside

In a separate large bowl, beat eggs.

Add pumpkin & sugar mixture to eggs. Stir well.

Slowly stir in evaporated milk.

Pour mixture into pie crust & bake for 15 minutes.

Reduce oven to 350 degrees & bake for additional 40-45 minutes or until a toothpick inserted near the center of pie comes out clean.

Remove from oven & cool on a wire rack for 2 hours before slicing. Serve immediately with fresh whipped cream or refrigerate to enjoy the following day.

"Cousin Love" Stephanie & Jessica

Smiles with Nani, Popi & Hunter

POPI'S FAVORITE APPLE PIE

Ingredients

8 apples (McIntosh, Cortland & Fuji are our favorites), *peeled & sliced*
2 tbs flour
¾ to 1 cup sugar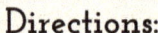
2 tsp cinnamon
¼ tsp nutmeg
dash of ground cloves
¼ cup butter
2 refrigerator pie crusts, *rolled flat*
additional 1 tsp cinnamon & 4 tsp sugar, *set aside for topping*

Directions:

Preheat oven to 425 degrees.

In a large pot, mix flour, sugar, cinnamon, nutmeg & cloves.

Add apples & stir until evenly covered.

Cook apple mixture on stove, stirring constantly until juices flow & apples are beginning to soften (about 5-7 minutes).

Remove mixture from stove & set aside.

Butter the bottom & sides of a pie dish then line with 1 pie crust.

Pour apple mixture into crust & dot with remaining butter.

Cover with second crust, tucking top crust under bottom crust & crimping/fluting edges before cutting 5 or 6 slits into top of pie to allow for steam to escape while baking.

Mix additional cinnamon & sugar, sprinkling on top of crust.

Bake for 15 min at 425, then lower oven to 350 & bake another 30-45 minutes or until apples are bubbly.

To keep crust from becoming too dark, use a ring of aluminum foil to cover edges during the last 15 minutes of baking.

Remove from oven. Let cool for 1 hour before serving.

If your apples are extra juicy & pie seems runny after cooling for 1 hour, refrigerate overnight & enjoy the following day.

POPI'S BIRTHDAY

While Popi's birthday (November 25) is always a big celebration, one of the most memorable parties by far was his 80th, which the family celebrated with a big Norsk theme.

Nani always manages to work Popi's favorite Norwegian dishes into a regular rotation along with her own family's Italian ones. But on Popi's birthday, it's all about our Head Viking.

OUR MENU

- Pork Schnitzel
- Balsamic Rosemary Carrots
- Venison Meatballs with Brown Gravy
- Grandma Avron's Potato Lefse
- Green Peas with Bacon
- Green Beans with Garlic

PORK SCHNITZEL

Ingredients

pork cutlets (Tip: ask your meat counter person to put them through the cuber)
2 eggs, well beaten
1 cup flour, seasoned with paprika, garlic powder, salt & pepper
1-2 cups plain bread crumbs
oil & melted butter

Directions:

Prepare your space for breading the meat with the flour mixture in one bowl, beaten eggs in another & breadcrumbs in a third.

Dip each pork cutlet into the flour mix, then eggs, then breadcrumbs.

Melt butter in a heated pan.

Fry each cutlet for 2-3 minutes on each side until golden brown.

Serve with a lemon wedge or mushroom gravy to make *Jaeger Schnitzel*.

Schnitzel is definitely one of Nani's signature dishes. There's something so magical about the way she prepares it with the perfect balance of crispy golden breading & tender meat. The flavors are so rich & savory because of the time & care she takes throughout the process. I always enjoyed the way she pounded the cutlets. Doing it with a funny little rhythm, almost like a dance. As of late, though, she's asked the butcher to tenderize each piece for her.

Every detail, from the seasoning she uses to the way the cutlets sizzle in the pan, reflects her love & attention, making a memory, a piece of tradition & a reminder of home.

-Jessica Greenlow (granddaughter)

"Norsk Smiles" Laura

BALSAMIC ROSEMARY CARROTS

Ingredients

1 lb carrots (large carrots sliced in half lengthwise or baby carrots left whole)
2-3 sprigs rosemary, chopped
2 tbsp balsamic vinegar
2 tbsp olive oil
salt & pepper to taste

Directions:

Preheat oven to 350 degrees.

Wash carrots & lay in a single layer on a cookie or shallow baking sheet.

In a small bowl, mix together vinegar, olive oil & rosemary.

Pour mixture over carrots, rolling to coat evenly.

Bake for 30-45 minutes or until carrots are tender.

Use What You Have

The pantry may be limited, but with a little creativity, you can make something delicious out of almost anything. This lesson teaches resourcefulness, improvisation & adaptability in both cooking & life.
-Nani

VENISON MEATBALLS WITH BROWN GRAVY

Ingredients

1 lb ground venison
½ lb ground pork
2 eggs
1 cup bread crumbs
1 medium onion, finely chopped
1 tbsp worcestershire sauce
1 tsp parsley
1 tsp paprika
½ tsp garlic powder
salt & pepper to taste
1 can broth, beef, chicken or vegetable
1 package leek soup mix or 1 can cream of mushroom soup
2 tbsp cornstarch *(to thicken gravy if desired)*
Optional: Use ground beef instead of venison.

Directions:

In a large bowl combine all ingredients except cornstarch, soup & broth.

Form into 20 meatballs.

In a large pan, fry over medium heat, turning frequently until browned on all sides

Add soup & broth to the pan with meatballs.

If necessary, add water so that mixture covers meatballs.

Cover pan with a lid & simmer until fully cooked. *(Internal temp for beef/pork 160 deg).*

Remove meatballs from the pan & set aside in a new dish.

To thicken gravy *(if desired)*, mix together in a small bowl, ¼ cup cold water & cornstarch until dissolved.

Add cornstarch slurry to gravy in pan & stir until desired consistency.

Pour gravy over meatballs & enjoy.

These are delicious fresh or frozen for future dinners. You can also make it Swedish by adding 1/2 cup of sour cream to the gravy & stirring until combined.

GRANDMA AVRON'S POTATO LEFSE

A traditional Norwegian flatbread. Delicious with butter & cinnamon sugar, or salmon, cream cheese & pickled herring.

Ingredients

3 cups russet potatoes, peeled, boiled & mashed or riced
1/2 cup cream or half & half
1/2 cup butter
2 tsp sugar
1/2 tsp salt
flour (amount will vary depending on dough consistency)

Directions:

Mix together all ingredients, slowly adding flour until dough reaches a solid form.

Cover & chill dough for 1-2 hours.

Form lefse dough into balls, approximately the size of a walnut or your palm.

Roll each ball out until paper-thin.

Bake on a hot griddle or pan until golden brown on both sides.

After baking, place a towel over the stack of lefsa or place inside a *Cuddler* to keep soft. Cool completely before storing in zip lock bags in the refrigerator or freezer.

Many hands make light work: Chelsea, Nani & DeeDee

Lefse making party: Jessica, Laura & Rob

Popi & Alana

GREEN PEAS WITH BACON

Ingredients

5 slices bacon, chopped & cooked
4 tbsp butter
1 large shallot, diced (or ¼ cup onion, diced)
1 clove garlic, minced
20 oz frozen green peas
1 tsp fresh thyme
2 tbsp water
salt & pepper to taste

Directions:

In a large skillet, cook bacon until browned & crisp.

Set bacon aside in another dish.

Add shallot to bacon fat & cook until tender, approx. 3-4 minutes.

Stir in garlic & thyme, cooking just until fragrant, approx. 1 minute.

Add frozen peas & 2 tbsp water to skillet, stirring to combine all ingredients.

Cover & cook over medium heat until peas are tender, approx. 4-5 minutes.

Remove the lid & cook until all liquid has evaporated.

Season to taste with salt & pepper. Sprinkle top with additional crispy bacon if desired.

GREEN BEANS WITH GARLIC

Ingredients

1 lb fresh green beans, trimmed
3 tbsp butter
3 garlic cloves, finely minced
salt & pepper to taste

Optional: swap out the garlic for another spice of your choice

Directions:

In a large saucepan, cover green beans with water & bring to a soft boil.

Reduce heat to medium-low & simmer for approx. 3-5 minutes.

Drain beans & rinse under cold water to stop the cooking process. Shake off any excess water.

In a large skillet over medium heat, melt butter, then add green beans & garlic.

Cook for 2 minutes until garlic has started to turn golden brown. Add salt & pepper to taste.

Transfer beans to a serving dish, serve & enjoy.

Growing up on the wall:
Popi, James & Hayden

Popi & Antheia

HOLIDAY TREATS

Nani & Popi are responsible for starting a number of traditions within our family, one of our favorites, though, is baking & giving away plates filled with a variety of cookies & treats.

Family, friends, extended family, the mailman, trash collector & anyone else that may cross Nani's path during the holiday season is sure to walk away with a plate full of goodies & a mason jar of Rumtopf. It's just another way she's able to spread joy & cheer, letting those she loves know how much they're appreciated.

OUR MENU

- Date Filled Cookies
- Sugar Cookies with Frosting
- Butter Balls *(aka Italian Wedding Cakes)*
- Pizzelles
- Crustella
- Pistachio Biscotti
- Filled Molasses Cookies
- Gingerbread Babies

- Chewy Almond Cookies
- Pecan Tarts
- Butter Toffee with Nuts
- Peanut Butter Fudge
- Spritz Cookies
- Kvikke Brod *(Norwegian Flatbread)*
- Peanut Butter Cookies
- Fattigmanns Bakkels
- Rumtopf

DATE FILLED COOKIES

Ingredients

3 cups dates, chopped
1 cup raisins
1 ¼ cup sugar
½ cup brown sugar
1 ½ cup water
3 cups flour, sifted
1 tsp baking soda
½ tsp salt
1 cup butter, softened
2 eggs
1 tsp vanilla

Directions:

In a medium bowl, cream together 1 cup sugar, brown sugar & butter.

Add eggs & vanilla. Beat well.

Carefully sift dry ingredients into bowl & mix well.

Cover & refrigerate for at least 2 hours.

While dough is chilling, in a medium saucepan, combine water, ¼ cup sugar, dates & raisins.

Bring to a boil & cook for 10 minutes, stirring occasionally.

Set aside & allow to cool.

Preheat oven to 375 degrees & separate dough into thirds.

On a lightly floured surface roll out ⅓ of dough at a time to approx. 1/16" thickness.

Cut into 2 inch rounds.

Place ½ tbsp of date mixture on half of the rounds, using another round to cover (like a sandwich).

Press edges together with a fork to seal.

Carefully transfer to a lightly greased cookie sheet & bake for 10-12 minutes until golden brown.

Optional: If desired, you can mix an egg wash & brush over cookies before baking for an added sheen & top with a sprinkle of sugar.

Everything Can Be Fixed or Forgiven
Burnt cookies or a soggy pie? It's never the end of the world. Mistakes are part of the process & they can always be salvaged or turned into something new like making crumbles from overcooked pie crust or using leftover roast for stew.
  -Nani

SUGAR COOKIES WITH FROSTING

Ingredients
Cookies:
2 & ¼ cups flour (plus more for rolling & work surface)
½ tsp baking powder
¼ tsp salt
¾ cup unsalted butter, softened to room temperature
¾ cup sugar
1 large egg, at room temperature
2 tsp pure vanilla extract
½ tsp pure almond extract

Frosting:
3 cups confectioners sugar
3-4 tbsp milk
1 ½ tbsp light corn syrup
1 tsp pure vanilla extract
pinch of salt

Directions:

In a medium bowl, whisk together flour, baking powder & salt. Set aside.

In a large bowl, beat together butter & sugar on high speed until smooth & creamy, approx. 3 minutes.

Add egg, vanilla & almond to sugar mixture, beating on high until combined, approx. 1 minute.

Add dry ingredients to wet ingredients & mix on low until combined. The dough will be a bit soft. If it seems too soft & sticky for rolling, add 1 more tbsp flour & combine.

Divide dough into 2 equal parts. Place each portion onto a piece of lightly floured parchment paper.

With a lightly floured rolling pin, roll dough out to approx. ¼ inch thickness.

Sprinkle more flour on surface & rolling pin if the dough seems too sticky.

The rolled-out dough can be in any shape, as long as it is evenly ¼ inch thick.

Lightly dust one of the pieces of rolled-out dough with flour.

Place a piece of parchment on top of floured dough & carefully lay 2nd rolled-out dough on top.

Cover with plastic wrap & refrigerate for at least 1-2 hours, up to 2 days.

When ready to bake, preheat oven to 350 degrees.

Line 2-3 large baking sheets with parchment paper.

Carefully remove top dough piece from the refrigerator. If it sticks to the bottom piece, carefully slide your hand under it to help.

Using a cookie cutter, cut the dough into chosen shapes.

Re-roll the remaining dough & continue cutting until all the dough is used.

Repeat this with the 2nd piece of dough.

Arrange raw cookies on baking sheets, approx. 2 inches apart.

Bake for 11-12 minutes or until lightly browned around the edges.

Allow cookies to cool on the baking sheet for a few minutes, then transfer to a wire rack to cool completely before decorating.

To make frosting:

In a medium bowl, mix all ingredients together. If frosting appears too thick, add 1 tsp of milk at a time to thin. If frosting appears too thin, add 1 tbsp of confectioners sugar at a time to thicken.

When cookies are fully cooled, carefully spread frosting on top of each cookie & allow to set.

My grandmother hasn't just taught me to follow a recipe, she's taught me the importance of infusing love, generosity, hope & good-will into everything I do. Nani never actually needs to reference a recipe like the rest of us do. There are so many things she can do simply by memory & feel. One of the things I enjoy the most about cooking is the process of things. A pinch of this, a dash of that. The memories I have, of being at Nani's side in the kitchen are truly some of my favorites.

I'm a very sensorial person, in large part due to my early experiences in the kitchen with Nani. The smells, the tastes, the touch, the experiences - they all combine to illuminate wisdom. Sure, the end result is always mouthwatering & delicious but the entire experience of being able to create wonder alongside my grandmother is the real magic.

-Jessica Greenlow (granddaughter)

BUTTER BALLS
aka Italian Wedding Cakes

Ingredients

1 ½ cups unsalted butter, softened
1 cup powdered sugar *(plus more for finishing)*
¼ tsp salt
1 egg, beaten
2 ½ tbsp water
1 ½ cups walnuts, chopped
2 tsp pure vanilla extract
3 cups sifted flour

Directions:

Preheat oven to 400 degrees & grease bottom of a cookie sheet.

In a large bowl, mix butter & powdered sugar with a wooden spoon until well combined.

Add egg, salt, water, nuts & vanilla. Mix well. Gradually stir in flour.

Roll into 1-inch balls & bake for roughly 15 minutes, until cookies are firm to the touch & pale golden in color.

While cookies are baking, pour extra powdered sugar into a medium bowl.

Immediately after removing from the oven, roll the cookies in powdered sugar. Let cool.

Once cooled, roll cookies through powdered sugar again to achieve a deeper frosting layer.

The Secret Ingredients are Laughter & Love

Christmas 1988: Chuck, Nani, DeeDee, Jessica, Popi, Nick & Mimi

PIZZELLES
Pronounced *'Piz-zel-lay'*

Ingredients

6 large eggs
1 ½ cups white sugar
1 cup unsalted butter, melted & cooled
1 ½ tsp pure vanilla extract
1 ½ tsp pure anise extract
3 ½ cups flour
4 tsp baking powder
½ teaspoon salt
confectioners sugar for dusting

Directions:

In a large bowl, beat eggs, sugar, vanilla & anise with an electric mixer until fluffy & smooth.

In a separate bowl, combine flour, salt & baking powder.

Gradually stir dry ingredients into the wet mixture

Stir in the melted butter until batter is smooth. Dough will be thick & sticky. Be careful not to over mix.

Preheat your Pizzelle iron according to the manufacturer's instructions. Lightly spray the iron with cooking spray & drop batter by 2 rounded spoonfuls onto the iron.

Close the lid & cook for approx. 90 seconds, until Pizzeles are golden or until steam stops coming out of the iron.

Carefully remove & allow to cool. Dust with confectioners sugar before serving. Store in an airtight container at room temperature.

CRUSTELLA

Ingredients

2 eggs
1 tbsp sugar
¼ tsp salt
1 cup flour
1 cup whole milk
1 tsp vanilla
oil for frying
powdered sugar

Directions:

In a large bowl combine eggs, sugar & salt. Beat well.

Add flour, milk & vanilla. Beat until smooth.

Heat a Crustella iron in 2-3 inches of oil to 365-375 degrees.

Carefully dip the hot iron into the batter. Make sure the batter only comes three-quarters of the way up the side of the iron.

Fry batter in the hot oil until golden brown.

Lift the iron out & allow excess oil to drain off.

Place the Crustella onto paper towels covering a wire rack.

Repeat the process of heating the iron, dipping it into the batter, frying & placing on paper towels to drain.

Sift powdered sugar over cooled Crustellas & enjoy.

The paper chimney & Chip

Popi & Antheia

PISTACHIO BISCOTTI

Ingredients

¾ cup white sugar
¼ cup light olive oil
1 ½ tsp vanilla extract
1 tsp almond extract
2 large eggs
1 ¾ cups flour
1 tsp baking powder
pinch of salt
1 ½ cups pistachio nuts
Optional: use almonds instead of pistachios if you prefer

Directions:

Preheat oven to 300 degrees & line a baking sheet with parchment paper.

In a large bowl, mix sugar & oil until well blended.

Add extracts & beat in eggs.

In a separate bowl, combine flour, baking powder & salt.

Gradually stir dry ingredients into the sugar mixture until thoroughly combined.

Fold in pistachios.

Divide dough in half, forming each half into a 12 x 2-inch log on a prepared cookie sheet. *If the dough is sticky, lightly wet your hands with water.*

Bake 30-35 minutes until light golden brown.

Remove from the oven & let cool for 30 minutes. *The biscotti will crumble if you try to cut them too soon.*

Once cooled, cut logs on the diagonal into ¾-inch thick slices & lay cut-side down on baking sheets.

Reduce oven temp to 275 degrees & bake for 8-9 minutes.

Sprinkle with powdered sugar or drizzle with melted chocolate.

Mark & I drove up to spend a few days at Nani & Popi's house for Thanksgiving 2024. When we arrived, the house already smelled amazing & was bustling with family, everyone doing something to help. I was honored when Popi asked if I'd like to accompany him to pick Nani up from her medical appointment. It gave us some great quality time together, which I cherish. To this day, observing the relationship between Nani & Popi is inspiring & absolutely heartwarming. They are both so extremely dedicated to ensuring the other feels loved & cared for in even the smallest of ways.

While that afternoon included countless last-minute trips to town, in search of key ingredients that had somehow been missed on previous excursions, eventually substitutions were obtained & in true Nani-form, everything was absolutely amazing. There's just something about the meals that come out of Nani's kitchen; you can taste the love in every bite.

Since losing my Mom, Dad & recently, my brother, these special moments spent with the family, at Nani & Popi's house, mean so much to me. I'm absolutely blessed to be a part of it. (Even if I am just the bean-dip & sub-roll getaway driver.)

-Kristine "Gretta" Costello-Avron (daughter-in-law)

FILLED MOLASSES COOKIES

Ingredients

½ cup shortening
½ cup packed brown sugar
1 egg
½ cup molasses
¼ cup buttermilk
3 cups flour
½ tsp salt
1 tsp baking powder
1 tsp cinnamon
¼ tsp ground cloves
¼ tsp nutmeg
¾ cup orange marmalade
approx 1 cup chopped dates, candied fruit, or raisins

Directions:

Preheat oven to 375 degrees.

Mix together shortening, sugar & egg thoroughly.

Stir in molasses & milk.

In a separate bowl blend together dry ingredients. Combine.

If dough is too soft to roll, cover & chill.

Divide dough into thirds.

On a lightly floured surface, roll dough (⅓ at a time) until 1/16 inch thick.

Cut into 2-inch rounds & place ½ of cut rounds onto a lightly greased baking sheet.

Top the rounds on the baking sheet with ½ tsp marmalade, then cover with remaining rounds & crimp together with a fork.

Place a piece of chopped date, candied fruit, or raisin on top of each finished cookie & bake for 10 to 12 minutes.

Makes approx 5 dozen, 2-inch cookies

3 Generations of Proud Bakers

GINGERBREAD BABIES

Ingredients

⅓ cup shortening
1 cup packed brown sugar
1 ½ cups dark molasses
⅔ cup cold water
7 cups flour
2 tsp baking soda
1 tsp salt
1 tsp allspice
1 tsp ground ginger
1 tsp ground cloves
1 tsp cinnamon

Directions:

Mix together shortening, sugar & molasses. Stir in cold water.

In a separate bowl blend all dry ingredients. Combine thoroughly. Cover & chill for at least 2 hours.

Preheat oven to 350 degrees.

Roll dough out on a lightly floured surface until it measures ¼ inch thick.

Cut with gingerbread boy & girl shapes & place 3 inches apart on a lightly greased baking sheet.

Bake for 10 to 12 minutes or until no imprint remains when touched lightly.

Makes approx 2 ½ dozen, 2 ½ inch cookies

CHEWY ALMOND COOKIES

Ingredients

2 egg whites
8 ounces almond paste
⅔ cup sugar
½ tsp salt
½ tsp vanilla
½ cup almond flour
confectioners sugar for dusting
sliced almonds

Directions:

In a medium bowl using a mixer, beat egg whites until frothy.

Add almond paste, sugar, salt & vanilla. Beat well.

Mix in almond flour, cover & refrigerate for 2 hours.

Preheat oven to 350 degrees & line 2 baking sheets with parchment paper.

Roll dough into 1-inch balls & place on lined cookie sheets, approx. 1-2 inches apart.

Lightly dust balls with confectioners sugar & press 2-3 sliced almonds into the tops.

Bake for 15-18 minutes, until edges are lightly golden brown.

Remove from the oven & cool on the baking sheet for 10 minutes before carefully transferring to a wire rack.

PECAN TARTS

Ingredients

Crust Dough:
4 ounces cream cheese, softened
½ cup butter, softened
1 cup flour
½ tsp salt

Pecan Filling:
¾ cup brown sugar
1 large egg, beaten
1 tbsp butter, melted
½ tsp vanilla extract
⅔ cups pecans, chopped

Directions:

In a medium bowl, mix together all crust ingredients. Form into a ball, cover with plastic wrap & refrigerate for 1 hour.

In a separate bowl, combine all filling ingredients.

Preheat oven to 350 degrees & prepare a mini muffin pan with cooking spray.

Divide crust dough into small balls & place into the greased muffin cups.

Carefully press dough into the bottom & sides of each muffin cup.

Fill cups with pecan filling & bake for 20 minutes or until crust is golden brown.

Allow to cool for 15-20 min in muffin tin, then remove & continue cooling on a rack.

BUTTER TOFFEE WITH NUTS

Ingredients

2 cups unsalted butter
2 cups sugar
¼ tsp salt
2 cups semisweet chocolate chips
1 cup almonds, walnuts, or pecans, finely chopped

Directions:

In a large, heavy-bottomed saucepan over medium heat, combine butter, sugar & salt.

Stir constantly in one direction until the butter is completely melted, approx. 5 minutes.

Line a 9 x 13-inch baking dish with parchment paper, allowing it to overhang on two sides of the dish.

Once the butter has melted, stop stirring & bring the mixture to a boil.

Cook, stirring only 2-3 times, until the mixture turns a dark amber color & the temperature reaches 285 degrees on a candy thermometer, approx. 20 to 30 minutes.

Immediately pour toffee into the prepared baking dish.

Sprinkle chocolate chips over the top & allow to set until they've softened, approx. 1-2 minutes.

Use a spatula to spread the softened chocolates into a thin, even layer.

Sprinkle nuts over the chocolate & press down lightly. *Hint: Wearing a plastic bag over your hand can help minimize the mess.*

Place pan in the refrigerator until set, approx 1 hour.

Lift hardened toffee out of the baking dish with the parchment paper & break into pieces.

Store in an airtight container.

sugar cookies with frosting

PEANUT BUTTER FUDGE

Ingredients

2 ½ cups sugar
½ tsp salt
½ stick unsalted butter
5 ounces evaporated milk (⅔ cup)
1 tbsp clear corn syrup
7 ½ ounces jar Marshmallow Fluff
½ tbsp vanilla extract
9 ounces peanut butter

Directions:

Line a 9-inch square baking pan with wax or parchment paper & set aside.

In a large saucepan over low heat, combine sugar, salt, butter, evaporated milk & corn syrup. Stir until blended.

Increase heat to medium & bring to a full-rolling boil. Be careful not to mistake escaping 'air bubbles' as a boil.

Boil slowly, stirring constantly for 3-5 minutes until *soft-ball stage* is reached.

The soft-ball stage is a test to see if the fudge has been cooked fully. Before you begin cooking, fill a small dish with ice water & set aside. After you've reached a full-rolling boil for 3½ minutes, dribble a few drops of the mixture into the ice water with a wooden spoon. After it cools in the water for approx. 10 seconds, you should be able to roll it into a small ball with your fingertips. If put in your mouth, it will be slightly chewy. If your fudge passes these tests, you are done with this step & should remove the mixture from the heat. Otherwise, cook for another 30 seconds & try the test again.

Cooking time will vary depending on humidity, altitude, cookware & cooktop temperature

Remove from heat, stir in peanut butter, vanilla & marshmallow fluff until mixed.

Turn the fudge into the prepared pan & cool.

Makes approx. 2½ pounds.

I knew that Judy was 'the one' from the very first moment I saw her. I was stepping off a bus to visit her for the first time after we'd had countless phone conversations & exchanged letters by mail. It wasn't long before we were out for an evening date & I just came right out & told her, "Judy, I want us to get married." I suppose that was what you'd consider my proposal & luckily, she agreed.

Our wedding day was extremely exciting. My favorite part though was her sitting beside me on the bench seat of our car. Just knowing that this was the beginning of our life together & that Judy would be right there beside me, for always. It didn't even matter that the windshield wiper was broken & kept getting stuck so I was constantly having to reach out the open window to push it back into rhythm. As far as I'm concerned, everything about that day was perfect.

Our first few months together as newlyweds weren't easy. We didn't yet have government quarters so we were stuck living out of suitcases at her sister Cathy's apartment, or Judy's folks' house. But still, none of that mattered. The little hiccups were nothing to worry about & we were able to maneuver them with ease. I believe those little tests only served to strengthen the love & connection we have with each other, preparing us for the lifetime ahead.

-Gordon 'Popi' Avron (husband, father, grandfather & great-grandfather)

SPRITZ COOKIES

Ingredients

1 cup butter, softened
½ cup sugar
2 ¼ cups flour
¼ tsp salt
1 egg
1 tsp almond or vanilla extract

Directions:

Preheat oven to 400 degrees & lightly grease the bottom of a baking sheet.

In a large bowl, beat together butter & sugar until mixed thoroughly.

Add all other ingredients & mix well.

Fill a spritz cookie press with dough & form shapes directly onto the baking sheet.

Bake for 5-7 minutes or until set but not brown.

Immediately remove cookies from the baking sheet & cool on a wire rack.

Optional: If you'd like to color your cookies, add a few drops of food coloring to the butter & sugar mixture before adding other ingredients.

KVIKKE BROD

(Norwegian Flatbread)

Ingredients

3 cups white flour
3 cups wheat floud
2 tsp salt
1 cup shortening
3/4 - 2/3 cups sugar
2 ½ cups buttermilk
1 tsp baking soda

Directions:

Preheat oven to 375 degrees.

In a large liquid measuring cup stir baking soda into buttermilk. Set aside.

In a large bowl combine flour, salt & sugar.

Cut shortening into dry ingredients.

Slowly add buttermilk until fully combined.

Divide dough into 6 even portions.

On a lightly floured surface roll each portion of dough into desired shape.

Dough will not rise while baking so roll out to desired thickness.

Carefully transfer to a lightly greased baking sheet.

Bake for 8-10 minutes or until desired crispness.

PEANUT BUTTER COOKIES

A word to the wise, these cookies disappear so it's never a bad idea to make a double batch. If you're feeling extra sweet, try using ¼ cup shortening & replacing the brown sugar with ½ cup honey for a delicious peanut butter & honey-flavored treat.

Ingredients

½ cup shortening
½ cup peanut butter
½ cup sugar
½ cup packed brown sugar
1 egg
1 ¼ cup flour
½ tsp baking powder
¾ tsp baking soda
¼ tsp salt

Directions:

In a large bowl, mix together shortening, peanut butter, sugars & egg.

In a separate bowl, blend dry ingredients.

Combine, cover & chill dough for at least 2 hours.

Preheat oven to 375 degrees.

Roll dough into 1 ¼ inch balls.

Place approx 3 inches apart on a lightly greased baking sheet.

Flatten balls in a crisscross style with the back of a fork that's been dipped in flour (this helps prevent it from sticking).

Bake for 10 to 12 minutes.

Makes approx 3 dozen, 2 ½ inch cookies.

Nani & Popi creating another happy home *(this one from fresh gingerbread)*

Santa's little helper

FATTIGMANNS BAKKELS

"Poor man's food" These Scandinavian fried cookies are rolled thin for a delicious crisp bite.

Ingredients

3 egg yolks
1 whole egg
½ tsp salt
¼ cup confectioner's sugar (powdered sugar)
1 tbsp rum flavoring
1 tsp vanilla extract
1 cup flour
lard, vegetable oil, or shortening for frying

Directions:

Heat a pan with 2 inches of lard, vegetable oil, or shortening until it measures 375 degrees.

Beat together eggs yolks, whole egg & salt until very stiff (approx 10 minutes).

Blend in confectioner's sugar & flavorings.

Add flour & mix well.

Knead dough on a well-floured cloth-covered board until the surface is blistered in appearance (approx 7 minutes).

Divide dough in half, rolling each half on a lightly floured surface until extremely thin.

With a pastry wheel or knife, cut dough into 4 x 2-inch diamonds.

Make a thin slit in the center of each diamond.

Draw a long point of each diamond through the slit, curling it in the opposite direction.

Fry until delicately brown (about 30 seconds) then turn over & brown the other side.

Carefully remove from pan & drain on an absorbent paper.

Sprinkle tops with confectioner's sugar before serving.

Makes approx 2-3 dozen cookies

In over 40 years, I can't say that I've ever had a bad meal from Nani's kitchen. She even makes a mean sandwich. Growing up, I came from a strictly meat & potatoes family, so it's been a real treat to experience the countless different cultural meals that she comes up with.

Whenever we get to Nani & Popi's house, the first place I go is the kitchen, just to see what she's making. No matter what time of day it is, there's always sure to be fresh coffee & cookies, especially for 3 o'clock coffee.

-Chuck Rice (son-in-law)

RUMTOPF

Making Rumtopf is an annual tradition in Germany, Austria & Denmark. For years, Nani & Popi gave away jars of Rumtopf to their closest family & friends along with a platter of sweet treats.

Ingredients

fruit (our family uses cherries, strawberries, red & black raspberries, etc)
80+ proof Dark Rum (750 ml per lb of fruit)
sugar (1 cup per lb of fruit)
a non-reactive crock with lid

Directions:

Wash & clean your fruit. If using larger fruits, be sure to trim them into smaller pieces.

In the bottom of your crock/jar, spread a layer of fruit.

Add a layer of sugar on top of the fruit.

Fill the jar with rum to fully cover the fruit & sugar.

If the fruit floats, use a small plate or bowl to weigh fruit down & ensure they remain covered with rum.

Cover with lid & store in a cool, dark place, such as a cellar or in the fridge.

Over the next few weeks, check the crock/jar, adding layers of fruit, sugar & rum as needed to refill. As the fruit begins to 'break down' the volume will naturally decrease.

Allow to process for 2-3 months, or longer.

Enjoy as a delicious topping on ice cream, pudding or cake. Or enjoy the fruit without anything & sip the rum. This can be delicious in a cup of tea, coffee, or hot cocoa.

Keep in mind that this is an obviously alcoholic drink & should be enjoyed responsibly by those over the age of 21. And please, be sure to never drink & drive.

Nani's Rumtopf Crock

CHRISTMAS EVE

Growing up in Nani & Popi's house, there would occasionally be a gift or two that were set aside to be opened early, on Christmas Eve. This was often something practical, but still special, like a fresh pair of Christmas pajamas or, if the family of 5 was headed to midnight mass, a new outfit for the occasion.

DeeDee recalls how exciting it was to slip into something new, knowing it had been chosen just for her. That simple pleasure made the moment feel even more magical.

OUR MENU

- Pizza Cheese Fondue
- Swiss Cheese Fondue
- Chocolate Crinkles

family reindeer games

PIZZA CHEESE FONDUE

Ingredients

1 tbsp extra virgin olive oil
1 garlic clove, minced
1 large block Velveeta cheese, cut into chunks for melting
½ cup Sauvignon Blanc wine (or another dry white wine)
1 small can of pizza sauce
crusty bread (French, banquette, sourdough, etc)
raw vegetables (carrots, celery, broccoli, cauliflower, zucchini, mushrooms, etc)
salt & pepper to taste

Directions:

Cut bread & vegetables into 1-inch squares.

In a fondue pot or saucepan, brown garlic in olive oil.

Add cheese & ¼ cup wine.

Cook on medium heat until the cheese has fully melted, stirring constantly.

Add pizza sauce & remaining wine, cooking & stirring until hot & fully combined.

Serve with raw vegetables & chunks of crusty bread (French baguette). *Our family likes to use cauliflower, broccoli, peppers (all colors), tomatoes, baby dill pickles, olives & mushrooms.*

Christmas Eve has always been special in our family. Every year, Nani, Popi, Mom, Dad, Jessi & I would pile into the car & head to 6 pm Mass. The church was always packed, with pews full of people in their best clothes. Something about that night always felt a little different, like time slowed down just enough to remind you to appreciate the holiday & your loved ones.

The real highlight came after we got home from church though. That's when the fondue pot came out. It was tradition, a bubbling pot of cheese surrounded by plates of bread, vegetables & meat. Each of us had our usual spot at the table & Nani always led the prayer, her words a little longer on Christmas, her gratitude more evident. Even as a kid, I could feel how much those moments meant to her.

Nick & Mom *(DeeDee)*

Then, the laughter started. If you dropped your bread or vegetable into the cheese, there was no getting out of it, you had to sing a Christmas Carol. No exceptions. We weren't exactly a family of talented performers, but that was half the fun. The off-key renditions & exaggerated performances that happened around Nani & Popi's table are some of my best memories.

Even now, we try to keep the tradition alive. Gathering at Nani & Popi's house, with 4 generations sitting around the table. Our kids making their own memories & our spouses trying desperately to plan their escape from 'the Carol rule.' I love knowing that one day, when our kids are older, they'll laugh about these memories & moments too.

-Nick Rice (grandson)

SWISS CHEESE FONDUE

Ingredients

1 garlic clove, halved
16 oz Gruyere Swiss cheese, shredded
8 oz another Swiss cheese (Fontina, Emmental), cut into chunks for melting
1 ½ tbsp cornstarch
1 cup Sauvignon Blanc wine (or another dry white wine)
1 tsp fresh lemon juice
pinch of Kirsch (optional)
pinch nutmeg
pinch pepper
crusty bread (French, banquette, sourdough, etc)
raw vegetables (carrots, celery, broccoli, cauliflower, zucchini, mushrooms, etc)

Directions:

Cut bread & vegetables into 1-inch squares.

In a fondue pot or saucepan, on medium heat, brown garlic in olive oil.

Add cornstarch, lemon juice & wine.

Whisk together until boiling, stirring constantly.

Add cheese & cook until fully melted.

Reduce heat to low & stir in spices.

Do not let the cheese come to a boil.

Serve & enjoy!

Growing up, Mom & Dad always made sure that Christmas was magic for us kids. I remember especially, the faux brick cardboard fireplace where our stockings hung. Oh, those stockings! They would hang, somewhat sadly on Christmas Eve, so empty, but then on Christmas morning, they were a sight, stuffed to the brim, sometimes even spilling over. There was always a tangerine tucked at the bottom, the bright orange peeking through holes of Grammie Lupo's crocheted stockings. Whole walnuts, striped candy canes, old-fashioned ribbon candy that looked like stained glass & solid chocolate Santas. Small trinkets, toys & other surprises filled every breath of space. The care that went into those stockings was a tradition of its own, one I carried on with my own children, hoping they would feel the same spark of wonder that I did every Christmas morning.

Mom & Dad have always made sure that the heart of our holidays wasn't just about the gifts. It was about the people. The love that filled our home was abundant, spilling over just like the stockings on our fireplace. And even now, as I continue these traditions with my own family, that love lingers in the glow of twinkling lights, the crackle of the fire flame for Christmas Cheese Fondue & the laughter that echoes through our celebrations.

This is how Christmas has always been: the gifts are sweet, the traditions are special, but Mom & Dad have always taught us that it's the people that make it magical. For that, I'll always be grateful.

-DeeDee Rice (daughter)

CHOCOLATE CRINKLES

Ingredients

½ cup vegetable oil
4 squares of unsweetened chocolate, melted (approx 4 oz)
2 cups sugar
4 eggs
2 tsp vanilla extract
2 cups flour
2 tsp baking powder
½ tsp salt
1 cup confectioner's sugar

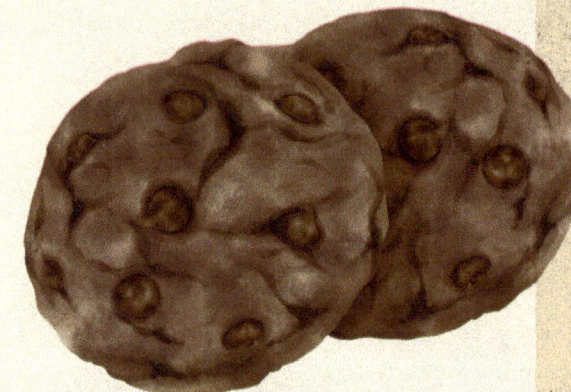

Directions:

Mix together oil, chocolate & sugar.

Blend in one egg at a time & vanilla, until well mixed.

In a separate bowl blend flour, baking powder & salt. Combine & mix well. Cover & chill for several hours, or overnight.

Preheat oven to 350 degrees.

Drop teaspoons of dough into confectioner's sugar, then remove & roll into balls.

Place approx 2 inches apart on a greased baking sheet.

Bake for 10 to 12 minutes. Keep an eye on these & be careful not to over-bake.

Makes approx 6 dozen cookies

When I went off to college, I bought a Better Homes & Gardens Cookbook, the same familiar red & white checked cookbook that Mom still has on her kitchen shelves today. What I liked about this cookbook was that there were dozens of blank pages in the back that I could fill with my favorite recipes from home. Mom's Italian Sauce, Mom's Chili, Mom's Mac 'n Cheese, Mom's Tuna Casserole, Mom's Soup Beans, Mom's Sheppard's Pie... These were my comfort foods & helped me feel at home even when away from the family.

My own family grew up with me making those same recipes & when they began their lives after college, I carefully copied Mom's recipes for them, adding Nani's to the title, where mine say Mom's, so they would remember where they came from. I still have that well-loved cookbook & every time I use it to make one of Mom's recipes, I'm brought back home to the feelings of Mom's kitchen.

Mom didn't just teach me how to find my way around the kitchen though, she taught me to be self-sufficient, how to do laundry at an early age so I wouldn't turn whites pink; she taught me how to use a sewing machine so that I could hem my pants & later, make my daughter's Halloween costume. Mom also shared with us kids her love for travel, adventure & experimenting with foods from cultures other than our own.

-Chip Avron (son)

CHRISTMAS MORNING

There are countless memories being made every year on Christmas morning. No matter your age, Nani & Popi always go out of their way to make sure you still feel the magic of the season.

One thing that sticks firmly with everyone in the family though, is the welcoming scent of Nani's Swedish Coffee Ring as it fills the kitchen & home. This is a treat that she bakes only once a year, on Christmas morning, a tradition that's been happening for as long as most of us can remember.

If you're looking for a delicious treat to add to your family's Christmas morning traditions, be sure to give the Swedish Coffee Ring recipe a try.

OUR MENU

- Swedish Coffee Ring
- Krumkake
- Breakfast Egg Bake

SWEDISH COFFEE RING

Ingredients

1 package active dry yeast
¼ cup warm water
¾ cup lukewarm milk
¼ cup sugar
¼ cup butter, softened
1 egg
½ tsp ground cardamom
½ tsp salt
3 ¼ to 3 ½ cups flour

Almond Filling:
½ cup almond paste
¼ cup packed brown sugar
¼ cup butter, softened

Directions:

In a large bowl, dissolve yeast in warm water. Allow to set for 5 minutes until foamy.

Stir in milk, sugar, butter, eggs, cardamom, salt & 2 cups flour.

Beat until smooth.

Slowly stir in the remaining flour until the dough is easy to handle.

Turn dough onto a lightly floured surface & knead until smooth & elastic, approx. 5 min.

Generously grease the inside of another bowl.

Place dough into the greased bowl, flipping so that the greased side is up.

Cover with a dishtowel & allow to rise in a warm place until the dough has doubled in size. (Approx. 1 to 1 ½ hours)

While dough is rising, prepare Almond Filling.

In a medium bowl combine all ingredients until smooth.

Set filling aside.

When the dough has doubled in size, punch down & pour out onto a lightly floured surface.

Using a rolling pin, spread the dough out into a 15x9-inch rectangle.

Cover evenly with filling & roll up tightly beginning on the long side of the rectangle.

Carefully move the roll onto a lightly greased cookie sheet & form into a ring.

Pinch the ends of the roll together to seal well.

With scissors, make cuts ⅔ of the way through the ring at 1-inch intervals.

Carefully turn each section on its side so the almond filling is visible.

Preheat oven to 350 degrees.

While preheating, allow the dough to rise until doubled in size.

Bake until golden brown, about 25-30 minutes.

There's so much to say about Mom & no where near enough time or space to share it all. So many memories, stories, meals & recipes.

So, instead of worrying about sharing the perfect story, I went to the recipe cupboard where our family's countless cook books live & pulled down the book that means the most to me. The one that holds pages bent & stained from so many years of use. And, without a second thought, I flipped right to a recipe that always makes me think of Mom.

The Swedish Coffee Ring, or "Tea Ring" as Mom calls it, is something she's been baking for Christmas morning for as long as I can remember. As a family, we spend the majority of our Christmas's together under one roof. Even when we were in the military, our homes were never far apart. On those occasions where we weren't able to celebrate together, Mom would still bake a Tea Ring & make sure that I had it to enjoy on Christmas Eve or Morning. To this day, I can close my eyes & smell it. Warm brown sugar, walnuts, cinnamon & butter.

When Mom knows that you love something, she always goes out of her way to make sure you have it for special occasions. It's not just the coffee ring, which tastes absolutely amazing, it's Mom, working hard in the kitchen to make sure her family experiences these continued traditions.

It's not just a delicious pastry, it tastes like Mom's love.

-DeeDee Rice (daughter)

KRUMKAKE

A popular Scandinavian delicacy perfect for the holidays.

Ingredients

4 eggs
1 cup sugar
½ cup butter, melted
5 tbsp heavy cream
1 tsp vanilla extract
¾ cup flour
2 tsp cornstarch

Directions:

Heat krumkake iron on medium-high heat.

Beat together eggs & sugar, then add butter, cream & vanilla. Mix thoroughly. In a separate bowl blend dry ingredients then combine. Mix until smooth.

Test krumkake iron with a few drops of water. If they 'jump,' the iron is ready to go.

Drop ½ tsp of batter onto an ungreased iron, then close gently. Do not squeeze.

Bake on each side for approx 15 seconds or until light golden brown. Keep iron over the heat at all times & do not be alarmed if the first few are slightly darker. The iron will cool slightly as it's used.

Remove from the iron with a knife & immediately roll onto a wooden roller.

Makes approx 6-7 dozen, 4-inch krumkakes.

Can be stored in a wax paper-lined container.

BREAKFAST EGG BAKE

Ingredients

3 cups frozen diced hashbrown potatoes
1 tsp olive oil
1 pound ground pork sausage
1 tsp dried rosemary
1 medium onion, chopped
2 garlic cloves, minced
1 bell pepper, chopped
1 cup mushrooms, sliced
1 cup fresh spinach, chopped
12 large eggs
1/4 tsp salt
1/8 tsp freshly ground black pepper
2/3 cup milk
1 cup shredded cheddar cheese
½ cup green onion, chopped

Directions:

Preheat oven to 375 degrees.

Grease the bottom & sides of a 9x13-inch baking dish.

Pour potatoes into the bottom of the dish in an even layer & set aside.

In a large skillet over medium heat, combine oil, sausage & rosemary.

Break sausage into bite-sized pieces as it cooks.

Add onion, garlic, peppers, mushrooms & spinach.

Cook for approx. 5-6 minutes.

Remove mixture from skillet & spread evenly over potatoes.

In a large bowl, whisk together eggs, salt, pepper, milk & cheese.

Pour over sausage mixture in dish.

Cover with aluminum foil & chill for at least 30 minutes, up to 24 hours.

When ready to bake, allow to sit at room temp for 10-15 minutes as the oven preheats.

Bake uncovered for 40-45 minutes.

Cool for 10 minutes before you slice & serve.

The Power of a Good Conversation

Some of the best talks happen while chopping vegetables or stirring a pot. This teaches the importance of slowing down & being present, sharing moments of connection with loved ones.
  -Nani

CHRISTMAS DINNER

Christmas at Nani & Popi's isn't just a single day, it's an entire season that begins the moment the first boxes of decorations come up from the cellar. The eclectic trinkets & treasures collected from travels abroad as well as things made by the children, grandchildren & now, great-grandchildren.

One memory that remains strong for all 3 grown-up Avron children *(Chip, Mark & DeeDee)* is the cardboard fireplace & chimney, with it's printed red bricks that faded over the years & it's single lightbulb delivering a flickering faux flame, where their stockings would be hung & filled with treasures, year after year, no matter where the family called home. Those same feelings of love, peace & joy continue to fill Nani & Popi's house today, not just on Christmas, but always..

OUR MENU

- Charcuterie Board
- Roast Beast & Gravy
- Nani's Famous Lasagna
- Scalloped Potatoes
- Roasted Brussels Sprouts
- Bacon Wrapped Asparagus
- Cheesy Garlic bread
- Pecan Pie

CHARCUTERIE BOARD
Also known as 'Rounds'

Ingredients

prosciutto
Italian cold cuts
pepperoni
dried sausages
Italian cheeses (Romano, Asiago, Roquefort or blue cheese)
cheddar cheese
assorted olives
stuffed sweet cherry peppers
artichoke hearts
fig jam
figs
assorted dried fruits
nuts
dipping oils
crusty breads
specialty crackers

Directions:

Get creative & arrange all ingredients on a large cutting board or platter.

The best Charcuterie Boards contain an assortment of flavors & delicious bites. The word charcuterie actually means 'cured meats' though, so in our family, sausage is a must.

You can include most anything you like, but a nice variety of fresh veggies, fruits, cured meats, cheeses, nuts & jams or oils are sure to keep everyone happy.

Nani's recipes are famous not only within our family but to the friends we prepare them for. I remember standing on a chair as a little girl while my Dad was making Nani's sauce, telling me what he was doing every step of the way.

Years later, when I moved in with James in California, we had roommates & I was proud to announce that I was Italian & a really great cook. When they told me to prove it, I reached out to Nani who quickly emailed me her sauce recipe. Today, when cooking for my family, I always measure with my heart, just like Nani does.

-Michelle Heath (granddaughter)

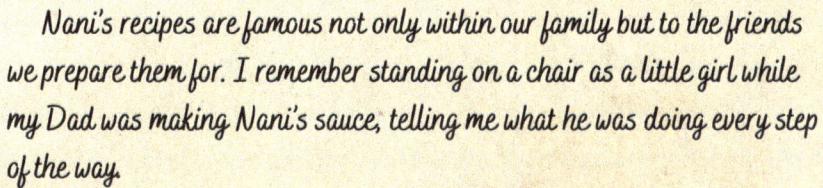

ROAST BEAST & GRAVY

Ingredients

2 tbsp olive oil
1 (8-10 pound) beef sirloin tip roast
1 medium onion, chopped
4 cloves garlic, minced
2 cups brewed coffee
3 cups water
3 cubes beef bouillon
6 fresh basil leaves
2 cups mushrooms, halved
1 tbsp salt
1 tsp ground black pepper
½ cup all-purpose flour
additional salt & pepper to taste.

Directions:

Heat oil in a large stock pot over medium heat.

Sear the roast in hot oil until slightly browned, approx. 2 minutes per side.

Carefully transfer the roast to a clean plate & set aside.

Add onion & garlic to the pot, stirring & cooking until onion is translucent, approx 10 minutes.

Return roast to the pot.

Pour coffee & 1 ½ cup water over the top of the roast.

Add bouillon, basil, salt & pepper, stirring to combine.

Bring to a boil then reduce heat to medium-low.

Cover & simmer until the meat is falling apart when pierced with a fork, approx. 2-3 hours.

Carefully transfer the roast to a serving dish & cover with a lid or aluminum foil.

Remove basil leaves from the pot.

Keep broth, onions & garlic in the pot over medium heat.

In a small bowl, whisk flour & remaining ½ cup water together until smooth.

Slowly whisk the flour mixture into the broth until the gravy is smooth & somewhat clear.

Season with salt & pepper as needed.

Pour about ½ of the gravy over the roast before serving & pour the rest into a gravy boat.

Enjoy with your favorite vegetables, mashed potatoes & crusty bread.

NANI'S FAMOUS LASAGNA

Ingredients

1 pot of Homemade Sauce (*see recipe for Grampie Lupo's Spaghetti Meat Sauce*)
1 box lasagna noodles

Filling:
2 cups mozzarella cheese
1 large container of Ricotta
1 cup parmesan cheese
4-5 eggs

Directions:

Preheat oven to 350 degrees.

Cook lasagna noodles until al dente

In a large bowl, mix all filling ingredients.

Cover the bottom of your pan with a thin layer of sauce.

Arrange one layer of noodles, then cover with another layer of sauce, and another later of noodles.

Spread half the filling mixture over noodle layer.

Arrange another later of noodles, sauces & more noodles.

Spread remaining filling mixture over noodles.

Continue layering with noodles & sauce until all noodles have been used, or pan is filled.

Sprinkle top with additional parmesan cheese & bake for 1 hour.

Cover with aluminum foil during last 20 minutes of baking to keep from drying out.

Let stand out of oven for 30 minutes or so before serving.

Serve with additional sauce if desired. This is one dish that tastes even better on day 2 or 3 once the flavors have all set up.

Mom's lasagna isn't just 'lasagna,' it's an 11-layer masterpiece. I've sampled lasagna at restaurants around the world but none of them have ever compared to Mom's.

Not too long ago Laura asked me for Nani's Lasagna recipe & because I was away on a business trip, I sent a quick text to Mom & in no time, she'd sent back a detailed how-to for perfect lasagna - without ever having to pause to check a cookbook or recipe card. Mom just 'knows' when it comes to anything in the kitchen.

-Chip Avron (son)

I love Nani's lasagna. It's the best. No restaurant will ever be able to compare. You just don't pass on Nani's lasagna & always take home leftovers if you get the chance.

-James Greenlow (grandson)

Mom's lasagna is incredibly delicious. As many times as I've made it over the years, following her exact recipe, it's still never quite like Mama's.

As the saying goes, "The secret ingredient is Mom's Love."

-DeeDee Rice (daughter)

SCALLOPED POTATOES

Ingredients

3 pounds Yukon gold potatoes, thinly sliced
½ medium onion, thinly sliced
9 tbsp flour
6 tbsp butter, softened & cubed
2 ½ cups milk
½ cup broth (vegetable, chicken or beef)
4 cloves garlic, minced
1 tbsp fresh thyme leaves, chopped
1 ½ cups grated cheddar cheese (*Nani always uses extra cheese if she knows that her Grandson James will be at dinner.*)
salt & pepper to taste

Directions:

Preheat oven to 400 degrees.

Grease the bottom & sides of a 9x13 inch baking dish.

In a small skillet over medium heat, melt the butter.

Add flour to the butter & whisk continuously for 1 minute.

Slowly add milk & vegetable broth, whisking steadily.

Once combined, add garlic & thyme, whisking often for 3 minutes. When it's ready, the sauce will lightly coat the back of a spoon.

Remove from the heat.

In baking dish, layer half of the potatoes along the bottom.

Next, layer on half of the onion, half of the sauce & 1 cup of cheese.

Repeat again with the remaining potatoes, onion, sauce & cheese.

Cover with aluminum foil & bake for 30 minutes.

Uncover & bake for an additional 35-40 minutes.

Let rest at room temperature for 20 minutes before serving.

ROASTED BRUSSELS SPROUTS

Ingredients

1 pound Brussels sprouts, trimmed
1 tbsp lemon juice
2 tsp fresh lemon zest
¼ cup grated Parmesan cheese
1 tbsp fresh thyme leaves, chopped
pinch of red pepper flakes
extra virgin olive oil
salt & pepper to taste

Directions:

Preheat oven to 425 degrees & line the bottom of a baking sheet or pan with parchment paper.

Cut Brussels sprouts in half lengthwise & place into baking sheet.

Drizzle sprouts with olive oil & a small sprinkle of salt & pepper.

Toss to evenly distribute & spread into a single layer.

Roast in oven for 20-30 minutes or under golden brown along the edges.

Before serving, toss sprouts with lemon juice, zest, parmesan cheese & fresh thyme.

Garnish with red pepper flakes.

Serve & enjoy.

BACON WRAPPED ASPARAGUS

Ingredients

1 pound fresh asparagus
10-12 slices bacon
2 tbsp butter, melted
¼ tsp garlic powder
1 tsp brown sugar

Directions:

Preheat oven to 400 degrees.

Wash & trim asparagus spears.

In a small bowl combine melted butter, garlic powder & brown sugar.

Dip each asparagus spear into butter mixture then wrap with a strip of bacon, leaving both the tip & end exposed.

Lay spears in a single layer on a cookie sheet or baking pan.

Repeat until all asparagus has been used.

Drizzle any remaining butter mixture over the top of the wrapped spears.

Bake for 20-25 minutes or until bacon is fully cooked.

If desired, place under the broiler for 3 minutes to crisp bacon.

Serve & enjoy!

CHEESY GARLIC BREAD

Ingredients

1 loaf of Italian or French bread
½ cup unsalted butter, softened
4 garlic cloves, minced
¼ tsp sea salt
2 tbsp chives, chopped
¼ cup Parmesan cheese, grated
¼ cup fresh mozzarella cheese, grated
red pepper flakes, optional

Directions:

Preheat the oven to 425 degrees & line a baking sheet with parchment paper.

Slice bread lengthwise & place cut side up onto baking sheet. Set aside.

In a medium bowl, mix together butter, garlic, salt & chives.

Evenly spread the butter mixture on both slices of bread.

Bake for 8 minutes until the edges are golden brown.

Carefully remove from oven & sprinkle bread with cheeses.

Bake for an additional 3 minutes until cheese is melted.

Sprinkle with red pepper flakes before serving if desired.

Slice & enjoy.

Growing up, spending time at Nani & Popi's always felt like an event. All of my Aunts, Uncles & Cousins would gather & yet somehow there was still always space at the table. Now, as an adult, one of the things I appreciate most about eating dinner at Nani & Popi's house is that after dinner & dessert are finished, the table has been cleared & the kids scatter to play, we adults continue to sit around the table & chat. Daily life can be hectic & busy, but when we're sitting at Nani & Popi's table, chatting & laughing together as a family, time seems to slow down.

I tell people that my Nani, my Dad & my fiancé Sean are the 3 best cooks I know. Sean loves to cook with Mexican flavors, something he learned from his own family & from working in their restaurant. At my daughter Paige's first birthday party, one of the most popular dishes was Sean's family's Mexican Mac & Cheese. Nani loved the dish & demanded to know why it hadn't been shared with her sooner. That year, when it came time to plan dishes for our family Christmas get-together, Nani decided on a Mexican theme, asking Sean to bring his famous Mac & Cheese. Wanting the dish to be fresh & absolutely perfect, Sean opted to take all of the necessary ingredients to Nani & Popi's house, to make it there. I remember standing at the edge of the room, watching Nani as she watched Sean. She simply couldn't stay out of the kitchen, needing to know everything he was doing, every step of the way. Nani loves watching others as they create in the kitchen, a space that will forever be the heart of her home.

There's no one quite like my Nani & Popi. They both have a way of 'filling my cup' whenever I see them. Those interactions, no matter how brief, leave me feeling loved, confident & special in a way that only the unwavering love of a grandparent can.

-Stephanie Avron (granddaughter)

PECAN PIE

Ingredients

1 pie crust, homemade or frozen
1 cup sugar
3 tbsp brown sugar
1/2 tsp salt
1 cup light corn syrup
1 tsp vanilla extract
1/3 cup butter, melted
3 large eggs
1 1/2 cups pecan halves

Directions:

Preheat oven to 425 degrees.

If using a homemade pie crust, place into 9x12 inch dish & refrigerate while preparing filling. If using a frozen pie crust, allow to rest on the counter instead.

In a large bowl combine sugar, brown sugar, salt, corn syrup & butter.

Mix in eggs & vanilla.

Stir pecans into the batter & pour into unbaked pie shell.

Use the back of a spoon to smooth top of the pie, moving pecans as needed to fill in any holes.

Bake at 425 degrees for 10 minutes.

Lower temperature to 350 degrees & bake for an additional 50 minutes.

Midway through baking, liberally grease one side of a large piece of aluminum foil & form a tent over the pie so that the crust is covered but the pie filling isn't being touched.

Carefully remove from the oven. The pie will be steady & not at all jiggly when done.

Allow pie to cool for several hours or refrigerate for up to 3 days.

Serve & enjoy with fresh whipped cream.

We moved around a bit when we were kids & joked that our family GMC Jimmy was home. Later in life, Nani and Papi's house became home. No matter where I've moved as I've gotten older though, their place still always feels like home. It's somewhere to rejuvenate & recharge your batteries before going back out into the world.

Whenever you start to feel depleted or tired, you can always count on Mom & Dad to feed your soul (& your belly). Simply being with the family for the holidays, birthdays, weddings, anniversaries, graduations, tea parties, or even just an uneventful Sunday dinner, you're surrounded by people who you love & who love you. There are no judgements, just love, support, lots of laughter & always food.

It warms my heart just thinking about it.

-Mark Avron (son)

Nani & Popi's Bench

ST. PATRICK'S DAY

In our family, we call this one a 'boiled dinner.' While our roots are primarily Italian & Norwegian, we can still make a mean Irish Stew, Corned Beef & Sauerkraut. Besides, there are some things that go beyond culture & history, like the desire to spend an evening with loved ones enjoying good food, loud laughs & a little storytelling magic.

OUR MENU

- Corned Beef, Cabbage & Potatoes
- Quick & Easy Sauerkraut
- Fermented Sauerkraut
- Guinness Beef Stew

CORNED BEEF, CABBAGE & POTATOES

Ingredients

1, 5-6 lb corned beef brisket
2 large onions, peeled & cut into wedges
8 carrots, peeled & cut into 1-inch pieces
2 heads of cabbage, cored & cut into wedges
10 small potatoes (yellow or red)

Directions:

Rinse brisket under cold water & place into the bottom of a large pot.

Place onion wedges on top of brisket & fill the pot with water.

Over medium heat bring to a boil & cook for 30 minutes.

Reduce heat to low, so the water remains at a gentle boil.

Cover the pot & cook for 3 ½ hours.

Add to the pot carrots, then cabbage & potatoes.

Cover & continue cooking until potatoes are fork-tender, approx. 30 minutes.

Remove all veggies from the pot & place into a serving bowl.

Slice corned beef brisket & enjoy.

QUICK & EASY SAUERKRAUT

This recipe will give you sauerkraut in under 30 minutes.

Ingredients

1 cup water
1 cup distilled white vinegar
½ onion, diced
1 head of green cabbage, cored & shredded
¾ tsp sea salt
2 tsp sugar
½ tsp celery seed
½ tsp onion powder
½ tsp garlic powder
black pepper to taste

Directions:

In a large pot over high heat combine all ingredients.

Cover & bring to a boil.

Reduce heat & simmer for 5 minutes.

Uncover & stir well to incorporate cabbage with other ingredients.

Recover & continue cooking, stirring occasionally, for 15 minutes or until cabbage is tender & wilted.

FERMENTED SAUERKRAUT

This recipe allows for approx. 2 weeks of fermenting for optimal flavor.

Ingredients

1 - 2 heads of fresh green cabbage
½ tsp sugar
½ tsp onion powder
½ tsp garlic powder
sea salt or kosher salt (2 tsp of salt for every pound of cabbage)

Directions:

Cut each cabbage head in half, remove the core, then slice very thinly. This can be done by hand with a knife, or using a mandolin. Be careful!

Weigh cabbage to determine how much salt will be needed.

Place sliced cabbage into a large bowl & sprinkle with salt.

Allow this to sit for approx. 20 minutes, until cabbage has started to wilt & release juices.

Using a tamper, pounder, or your hands, crush the cabbage until it's further wilted. This can take a few minutes.

Transfer the cabbage & all juices to mason jars. The cabbage should be completely submerged under the brine. If necessary, combine 1 tsp salt in 1 cup water & add to the jars to fully cover the cabbage.

Firmly close jars & store them in a dark place, a basement or kitchen pantry is perfect.

You can begin taste testing your sauerkraut after 4 days but it's recommended that you allow the fermentation process to do its magic for 2 weeks for optimum tanginess.

Once your sauerkraut is finished, it can be stored in the fridge for up to 3 months.

A Pinch of Love

Cooking with love is what makes the difference between an ordinary meal & one that becomes a cherished memory. The intention & care you put into your work is what makes it special.
  —Nani

GUINNESS BEEF STEW

Ingredients

3 tbsp olive oil, divided
3 lbs beef chuck roast, trimmed & cut into bite-size pieces
6 oz bacon or speck, diced
2 medium onions, diced
4 cloves garlic, minced
1/4 cup all-purpose flour
3 large carrots, peeled & cut into bite-sized pieces
2 celery stalks, cut into bite-sized pieces
1 1/2 lbs potatoes, peeled & cut into bite-sized pieces
14 oz Guinness beer
4 cups beef stock or broth
3 tbsp tomato paste
2 tbsp Worcestershire sauce
2 whole bay leaves
1 tbsp dried thyme
salt & pepper to taste

Directions:

Pat beef dry with a paper towel then season with salt & pepper.

Pour 1 ½ tbsp oil into the bottom of a large stockpot over high heat.

Add ½ of the beef & brown on all sides, creating a nice sear/crust.

Remove beef from the pot & set aside on a clean plate.

Repeat with remaining oil & beef.

Lower heat to medium.

Add a splash of oil to the pan along with garlic & onion.

Sauté for 3 minutes.

Add bacon & cook until browned.

Stir in carrot, celery & potatoes.

Add flour & stir for 1 minute.

Slowly pour Guinness, broth, Worcestershire sauce & tomato paste into the pot, mixing well until the flour has fully dissolved.

Add bay leaves & thyme.

Carefully return all beef to the pot. Liquid should cover all ingredients; if not, additional broth can be used.

Cover the pot & simmer on low for 1 ½ hours, stirring occasionally.

Stew will be finished when beef is tender to the touch & potatoes are softened.

Remove bay leaves & add salt & pepper to taste.

Serve & enjoy with a large hunk of crusty bread & butter.

MOTHER'S DAY

In our family, Mother's Day is an extremely important holiday to celebrate. No doubt because of how much we all love & respect our maternal head of the family, Nani, but also for the other amazing moms within the family.

We celebrate the day with brunch, which involves making dozens of crêpes every year, from scratch of course, flowers, sweet treats & seemingly endless laughter.

OUR MENU

- Crêpes
- Brunch Quiche
- Spanakopita
- Sweet Ricotta Pie

CRÊPES

Ingredients:

Crêpes:
4 large eggs
1 cup milk
1 cup water
1 ¼ cups all-purpose flour
3 tbsp butter, melted + more for cooking
½ tsp salt

Raspberry Blueberry & Strawberry Compote Filling:
2 cups fresh or frozen berries
1 tbsp lemon juice
2 tbsp sugar
2 tbsp water

Directions:

Crêpes:
Combine all ingredients in a blender on high speed for 1 minute.

Let crêpe batter sit at room temperature for 1 hour. (You can also chill it overnight in the fridge.)

Preheat a 6-7 inch nonstick skillet over medium heat.

When hot, melt 1 tsp butter in skillet.

Using a ¼ cup measuring cup, pour the batter into the center of the skillet, moving the skillet so the batter spreads evenly to the edges.

Cook only until the surface is bubbly, then carefully flip using your fingers or a spatula.

Allow to cook on the other side until golden brown.

Carefully move the crêpe from the skillet to a clean plate.

Cover with a tea towel to keep warm.

Repeat the process until all crêpes have been finished.

Fillings:
Combine all ingredients in a heavy saucepan.

Bring to a boil & allow to cook for 5 minutes.

Reduce heat & simmer for 10 minutes, stirring occasionally.

Compote will thicken as it cools.

Hint: If your compote is not as thick as you'd like, add 1 tsp cornstarch & bring back to a boil.

Evenly distribute filling into each crêpe, gently rolling into a log shape.

Our family has also been known to fill crêpes with a generous helping of chocolate hazelnut spread on special occasions.

BRUNCH QUICHE

Ingredients

1 unbaked pie crust
4 large eggs
½ cup whole milk
½ heavy cream
¼ tsp salt
¼ tsp pepper
¼ tsp ground mustard
1 cup shredded or crumbled cheese
(feta, cheddar, goat cheese, or gruyere)
2 cups of your favorite filling items
(ie. chopped ham, broccoli, peppers, onions, mushrooms, salmon, bacon, sausage, etc)

Directions:

Preheat oven to 400 degrees.

In a large bowl beat eggs, whole milk, heavy cream, salt, pepper & ground mustard together until completely combined, about 1 minute. Set aside.

Sprinkle ½ cup of cheese & 1 cup of filling items into the bottom of the pie crust.

Pour egg mixture into the crust & sprinkle with remaining cheese & filling items.

Bake for 45-55 minutes on a baking sheet, until center is set.

Allow to cool for 15 minutes before slicing & serving.

When I think of Nani, I think of her warm hugs, her soul-cooked food made with love, her contagious laugh & infectious smile. She's always been there, during the biggest moments in my life & I'm forever grateful that she's shared those times with me.

The relationship between Nani & Popi is something truly magical. Seeing how much love they still share for each other after 60+ years together is an inspiration to all of us. The home & family they've created is one filled with peace, love, happiness & comfort.

Everyone deserves to have a Nani like mine in their lives & I pray she knows how amazing, beautiful & important she is to all of us.

-Chelsea Henggeler (granddaughter)

SPANAKOPITA

Ingredients

Filling:

16 oz frozen chopped spinach, thawed & drained
4 tbsp parsley, chopped
1 large onion, finely chopped
2 garlic cloves, minced
2 tbsp extra virgin olive oil
4 eggs
10.5 oz feta cheese, crumbled
2 tbsp fresh dill, chopped
salt & pepper to taste

Crust:

1-18 oz package of phyllo dough, thawed & laid flat
1 cup olive oil

Directions:

Preheat oven to 325 degrees.

In a large bowl mix all filling ingredients until well combined.

Unroll the phyllo sheets & place them between 2 slightly damp kitchen towels.

Brush the bottom & sides of a 9x13-inch baking dish with olive oil.

Line the baking dish with 2 sheets of phyllo, brushing the sheets with olive oil.

Repeat this 5 times, until you've used 10 sheets of phyllo.

Evenly spread the filling mixture into the dish.

Top with 2 sheets of phyllo & brush with olive oil.

Repeat this until all phyllo sheets have been used.

Brush the top layer of phyllo with olive oil & sprinkle lightly with a few drops of water.

Carefully fold or crinkle any excess phyllo that reaches outside the dish back towards the center.

Brush these folded side pieces with olive oil.

Bake for 1 hour, until the phyllo is crisp & golden brown. Remove from the oven & allow to set for 10 minutes before cutting.

Serve & enjoy!

Chip, DeeDee & Mark yodeling in the Swiss Alps

SWEET RICOTTA PIE

Ingredients

Crust:
2 cups flour
½ cup confectioner's sugar
¼ tsp baking powder
1 cup unsalted butter

Filling:
32 oz whole milk ricotta
¾ cup sugar
4 large eggs
1 tsp lemon juice
1 tsp fresh lemon zest
½ tsp vanilla extract
1 tsp almond extract

Topping:
orange liqueur
sliced almonds
sugar

Directions:

Preheat oven to 350°F

For the crust:
In a large bowl, cream butter & confectioners' sugar until light & fluffy.

Stir together flour & baking powder; blend into butter mixture.

Pat crust into the bottom of a 9-inch pie plate.

For the filling:
Mix together all filling ingredients & pour into pie crust.

Bake until a knife inserted into the center comes out clean, about 40 minutes to 1 hour.

Remove pie from the oven & top with almond slices.

Brush top with orange liqueur & sprinkle with sugar.

Allow to cool before serving.

Nani & Baby Keegan

Nani, Jessica & Stephanie on the way to a Luke Bryan Concert

Growing up as kids we always got a kick out of how Mom would purse her lips when she was preparing a meal, sometimes even showing a little tongue, a habit she still has today. While Mom loves taking her time seasoning & tasting whatever amazing dish she's creating in the kitchen, when it comes time to eat, there's no dawdling. Mom likes her meals served hot! Once everyone has taken their seat, Mom leads us in a blessing, thanking God for the day & then, it's time to enjoy.

Mom has a way of remembering what every family member likes & dislikes when it comes to their favorite meals. She put so much extra care into making sure every person feels loved, it's amazing how she manages to remember us all. As her family continues to grow, so has her dining room table. Over the years I've asked Mom for countless recipes to make at home for my own family, especially those that were passed down from her own parents, like 'The Sauce' & of course her incredible lasagna.

Mom has always instilled in us the importance of family & sharing meals together. The love & conversation shared around our family dinner table is always absolutely priceless. I'm forever grateful for my Mom; the way she cares for, believes in & unconditionally loves everyone within her family.

-DeeDee Rice (daughter)

FATHER'S DAY

Father's Day brings sunny weather & a full day spent outside sitting in Nani & Popi's beautiful backyard. We cook on the grill, eat until our bellies are full & share countless stories & memories about Popi, our father, grandfather & great-grandfather, as well as the other amazing Dads within our family.

This day is special, an opportunity for each of us to give thanks to our Dads for the many ways in which they've helped take care of us & keep us safe over the years.

OUR MENU

- Grilled Steak Skewers
- Grilled Chicken Breasts
- Fresh Fruit Salad
- Greek Salad

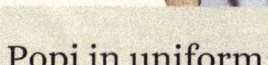

Popi in uniform

GRILLED STEAK SKEWERS

Ingredients

Marinade:
¼ cup olive oil
¼ cup soy sauce
1 ½ tbsp lemon juice
1 ½ tbsp red wine vinegar
2 ½ tbsp Worcestershire sauce
2 tbsp honey
1 tsp onion powder
2 tsp Dijon mustard
2 cloves garlic, minced

Kebabs:
2 lbs sirloin steak, cut into 1 ¼-inch pieces
8 oz button mushrooms, halved
1 pineapple, cut into 1 ¼-inch chunks
3 bell peppers (1 red, 1 green, 1 yellow), cut into 1 ¼-inch pieces
1 red onion, cut into 1 ¼-inch chunks
1 tbsp olive oil
½ tsp garlic powder
10 wooden skewers, soaked in water for at least 30 minutes
salt & pepper to taste

Directions:

In a medium bowl, combine all marinade ingredients. Set aside.

In a large resealable bag, combine steak pieces & marinade.

Seal the bag, pressing out any excess air & softly massage the marinade to evenly coat the meat.

Place the resealable bag into the fridge & allow the meat to marinate for 3-6 hours.

When ready to prepare, preheat the grill to medium-high heat, approx 425 degrees.

While the grill is preheating, place all veggies & pineapple into a large bowl.

Drizzle veggies with olive oil & garlic powder.

Carefully stir to evenly coat without breaking down the veggie pieces.

Assemble skewers by layering pieces of veggies, steak & pineapple.

Brush the grates of your grill lightly with olive oil & place skewers on the grill, turning every 8-9 minutes.

Skewers are done when the steak shows a temperature of 140-145 degrees with a meat thermometer.

Serve & enjoy.

Popi at work. Vicenza, Italy 1969

GRILLED CHICKEN BREASTS

Ingredients

2 lbs boneless, skinless chicken breasts
6 tbsp extra virgin olive oil
4 garlic cloves, minced
3 tbsp brown sugar
1 tsp dried thyme
½ tsp dried oregano
½ tsp onion powder
2 tsp cayenne pepper
1 tsp salt
¼ tsp freshly ground black pepper

Directions:

One at a time, place chicken breasts in a large resealable bag.

Using a meat mallet, rolling pin, or the bottom of a pot, carefully pound each breast to approx. ½-inch thickness.

Set all flattened breasts aside on a plate or cutting board.

In a large bowl combine all other ingredients & mix well.

One of by one, add chicken to the bowl, evenly coating with the spice mixture.

Move chicken & all seasonings from the bowl into a large resealable bag. Seal & place into the fridge to marinate.

Chill for at least 3 hours or overnight.

When ready to prepare, preheat the grill to high heat & lightly brush the grates with oil.

Place the chicken breasts on the grill & cook, covered for approx. 2-3 minutes per side.

The chicken will reach 165 degrees when measured with a meat thermometer when done.

Serve & enjoy.

Servicemen in the News!

SGM Gordon H. Avron, son of Martha and the late Odin Avron, Middle River, has attained the highest rank of enlistment in the U.S. Army. He was promoted to Sergeant Major on October 1, 1985. He has been stationed at the Picantinny Arsenal in Dover, New Jersey, for the past year. Prior to that he attended the Sergeants Academy, Fort Bliss, Texas. SGM Avron, was transferred to Vilseck, West Germany, on November 20 for three years.

FRESH FRUIT SALAD

Ingredients

1 pound grapes, red or green
2 cups fresh pineapple, chopped
1 pound strawberries, sliced
6 oz blueberries
6 oz blackberries
3 kiwis, sliced
½ cup pineapple juice
2 tbsp fresh lime juice
2 tbsp local honey
zest of 1 lime

Directions:

Carefully combine all ingredients into a large mixing bowl. Be sure that everything is tossed evenly to coat.

Serve & enjoy!

Nani, Popi & baby Hayden

GREEK SALAD

Ingredients

1 cucumber, thinly sliced
3 Roma tomatoes, chopped
1 green pepper, diced or cubed
1 red pepper, diced or cubed
1 red onion, sliced
Greek black olives
1 avocado, cubed
8 oz feta cheese chunks
1 clove garlic, finely minced
2 tsp lemon juice
1 tsp parsley
3 tbsp olive oil
2 tbsp red wine vinegar
1 tsp oregano
3 tbsp honey
salt & pepper to taste

Directions:

In a large bowl mix together garlic, lemon juice, parsley, olive oil, red wine vinegar, oregano & honey.

Add cucumber, tomatoes, peppers, onion & olives to the bowl & stir to coat evenly.

Stir in avocado & feta cheese.

Cover & refrigerate until ready to eat.

INDEPENDENCE DAY

As with most other families in America, ours celebrates the 4th of July with plenty of dishes coming from both in the kitchen & off the BBQ Grill. We gather most often in Nani & Popi's backyard to enjoy the sun & fun before the younger kids go back to school in the Fall.

OUR MENU

- BBQ Hamburgers
- Baked Beans
- Coleslaw
- Pasta Salad
- Potato Salad

BBQ HAMBURGERS

Ingredients

2 lbs 80/20 lean ground beef
2 cloves garlic, minced
3 tbsp onion, minced
½ tsp ground mustard
1 tbsp Worcestershire sauce

Rare: approx. 4 minutes or 125 degrees.
Medium-Rare: approx. 5 minutes or 135 degrees.
Medium: approx. 6-7 minutes or 145 degrees.
Well-Done: approx. 8-9 minutes or 160 degrees.

Directions:

In a medium bowl combine all ingredients.

Using your hands fold all ingredients together until combined.

Be careful not to over mix.

Divide mixture into 6 even portions.

Carefully form each portion into a patty approx. 4 inches across.

Hint: If you leave the outer edges of each patty slightly thicker than the center, it'll help them remain flat while cooking.

Place patties on a baking sheet covered with parchment paper, cover with plastic wrap & refrigerate for up to half an hour before grilling.

Cook patties on a 450-500 degree grill, flipping at least once, until they reach your desired temp.

Serve on a lightly toasted bun, topped with sliced cheese, lettuce, tomatoes, pickles & onion.

BAKED BEANS

Ingredients

2 cans baked beans (your choice of brand)
½ cup brown sugar
½ onion, chopped
¼ cup each catsup & mustard
3 strips bacon, cooked & crumbled

Set aside: 3 strips bacon, cooked

Directions:

Preheat oven to 350 degrees.

In a large baking pan, mix together all ingredients except for 3 strips of bacon that have been cooked & set aside.

Bake 30-40 minutes.

Everything Has a Purpose

Leftover vegetable scraps or an old loaf of bread, everything in the kitchen can be repurposed. In life, nothing is wasted; every experience, every challenge & every moment has value, even if we don't always see it right away. Keep asking yourself, "what else is possible?"
  -Nani

COLESLAW

Ingredients

¼ cup mayonnaise
2 tbsp sugar
2 tbsp milk
2 tbsp apple cider vinegar
2 tbsp Dijon mustard
1 medium cabbage, shredded
salt, pepper & celery seed, to taste

Directions:

Mix mayonnaise, sugar, milk, vinegar & mustard together.

Stir in cabbage & refrigerate for at least 1 hour.

Season with salt, pepper & celery salt to taste before serving.

Swim lessons at Nani & Popi's pool

PASTA SALAD

Ingredients

1 pound dried pasta *(fusilli, penne, rotini, or farfalle)*
1 medium bell pepper, chopped
1 cup cucumbers, sliced & quartered
1 ½ cups cherry tomatoes, halved
1/3 cup green onions, chopped
2 cups arugula, chopped
1 ½ cups chickpeas, drained & rinsed
1 cup olives, halved
1 ½ cups crumbled feta cheese
1/2 cup fresh basil, chopped
¼ cup toasted pine nuts
1/3 cup red wine vinegar
¼ tsp red pepper flakes
1/2 cup extra-virgin olive oil
salt & pepper to taste

Directions:

Bring a large pot of salted water to a boil. Add pasta & cook until tender, approx. 6-10 minutes.

While pasta is cooking, in a large bowl whisk vinegar, red pepper flakes, ground black pepper & olive oil until blended.

Drain pasta & rinse well under cold water.

Stir in bell pepper, cucumber, tomatoes, onions, arugula, chickpeas, olives, feta cheese, basil & pine nuts until fully combined. Season with salt & pepper as needed.

Cover & refrigerate for at least 30 minutes before serving.

Mark & Nani

Nani & Popi showing the kids how it's done

POTATO SALAD

Ingredients

3 pounds potatoes, washed & cut into ¾ inch cubes
2 1/2 teaspoons kosher salt, divided, plus more as needed
3 hard-boiled eggs, diced
4 oz gouda cheese, cut into ¼ inch cubes
3 dill pickle spears, chopped
2 celery stalks, chopped
1 large shallot, chopped
2 green onions, chopped
2 tbsp fresh dill, chopped
1 ¼ cup mayonnaise
1 tbsp Dijon mustard
2 tbsp apple cider vinegar
salt & pepper to taste

Directions:

In a large pot over high heat, add potatoes & 2 tsp salt. Fill with water until potatoes are covered, plus 1 inch.

When water reaches a boil reduce heat to medium to maintain a gentle simmer.

Cook potatoes until they are fork-tender, approx 8-10 minutes.

While potatoes are cooking, in a medium bowl combine hard-boiled eggs, pickles, celery, shallot, onion & dill.

Add mayonnaise, mustard & 1 tbsp vinegar. Stir to combine.

Drain potatoes & spread them into a single layer on a baking sheet/dish.

Sprinkle remaining vinegar over the potatoes & allow to cool to room temp, approx. 15 minutes.

Add gouda cheese & potatoes to the bowl & mix well.

Season with salt & pepper as needed.

Cover & refrigerate for at least 1 hour before serving.

When I met Nani for the first time, she immediately accepted me as another of her many grandchildren. Now, I'm blessed to see the relationship she has with my own children, her great-grandchildren, strengthen & grow every single day.

The indescribable bond between Nani, Popi & my kids fills my heart with so much joy. Especially Hunter. Their connection is simply magic. Nani is true strength, courage & love.

-Carrisa Kotsopoulos (granddaughter)

My favorite thing about Nani is that she plays dinosaurs with me. I like that a lot.

-Hunter Rice (great-grandson)

NANI'S BIRTHDAY

Our family goes all out when it comes to celebrating our Nani. Every year finds us focused on a new theme, from Hawaiian Luau to High Tea & everything in between. But, the fun doesn't stop there. After a nice afternoon luncheon, without fail, we spend the evening together around the same big table at Nani & Popi's house, for a pot of Homemade Sauce while Nani & Popi retell our favorite stories about their lives & countless adventures.

OUR MENU

- Open-Faced Salmon Finger Sandwiches
- Cucumber Sandwiches
- Chewy Molasses Cookies
- Canadian Oatmeal Shortbread

OPEN-FACED SALMON FINGER SANDWICHES

(this recipe makes 16 small finger sandwiches)

Ingredients

1/4 cup sour cream
4 oz goat's cheese, softened
2 tsp fresh dill weed, chopped
1 tsp lemon juice
4 slices thinly-sliced marbled rye bread (or bread of choice)
7 oz smoked salmon
2 tbsp capers
1 tbsp fresh chives, chopped
small handful of micro greens

Directions:

Trim crust & edges from slices of bread. Cut each slice into 4 smaller square pieces.

Slice salmon into 16 even ribbons & set aside.

In a bowl or food processor, combine sour cream, goat's cheese, chopped dill weed & lemon juice.

Spread sour cream mixture evenly onto bread slices.

Top each slice with a small bunch of micro greens & 1 piece of salmon.

Garnish with capers & chives.

Serve immediately.

CUCUMBER SANDWICHES

Ingredients

8 oz sour cream
2 tsp fresh dill, chopped
2-4 tsp fresh lemon juice
1 English cucumber, thinly sliced
1 loaf thinly sliced white bread
salt & pepper to taste
Optional: thinly sliced fresh salmon

Directions:

In a medium bowl, combine sour cream, fresh dill & lemon juice.

Thinly slice cucumbers. Sprinkle lightly with salt & pepper. Set aside.

Spread the mixture onto one side of all bread slices.

Layer cucumber slices over half of the bread slices.

Top with remaining bread slices.

Trim crusts & cut each sandwich diagonally to create 4 small triangles.

Serve immediately or cover & store for up to 24 hours.

CHEWY MOLASSES COOKIES

Ingredients

⅓ cup shortening
½ cup sugar
2 eggs
½ cup molasses
1 tbsp milk
1 ¼ cups flour
1 tsp baking soda
½ tsp salt
½ tsp cinnamon
¼ tsp ground cloves
¼ allspice
1 cup currants
½ cup chopped nuts of your choice
2 tsp vanilla extract

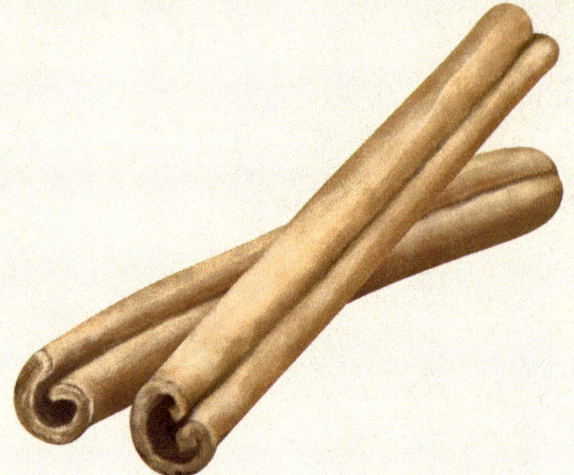

Directions:

Cream together shortening & sugar thoroughly.

Stir in eggs, molasses & milk - blend well.

In a separate bowl, blend together dry ingredients.

Combine, adding currants, nuts & vanilla extract.

Mix well. Cover & chill for several hours until firm.

Preheat oven to 350 degrees.

Drop dough in small teaspoonfuls approx. 2 inches apart on a well-greased baking sheet.

Bake for 15 minutes.

Allow to cool for a few moments before moving to a cooling rack.

Makes approx 4 dozen, 2 ½ inch cookies

Spending time with Nani & Popi is always comfortable. From the very first time I met them, I felt accepted & loved. Some of my favorite memories with them are the quiet moments, after big meals when we just get to sit & talk; hearing them share stories about their lives.

I know that I'll always remember Nani's birthday tea party though. She wanted to celebrate her birthday & to do it big with the entire family there. It was so much fun watching Nani, as she sat back & watched everyone having such a good time. That's such a big part of who Nani is; she's always concerned about making sure the people she loves are taken care of & having the best possible time.

-Rob Henggeler (grandson)

CANADIAN OATMEAL SHORTBREAD

These are popi's favorites & they taste even better after being stored for 24-hours, if they last that long.

Ingredients

1 cup butter (melted)
½ cup packed brown sugar
1 tsp vanilla extract
1 cup flour
½ tsp baking soda
2 cups rolled oats

Directions:

Mix together butter, sugar & vanilla until fluffy.

In a separate bowl, blend flour, baking soda & oats.

Combine, cover & chill for 1-2 hours.

Preheat oven to 350 degrees.

Roll out dough on a lightly floured surface until ¼ inch thick.

Cut into squares or shapes using cookie cutters.

Bake on an ungreased baking sheet for 10-12 minutes.

Makes 3 ½ -4 dozen cookies

EVERYDAY RECIPES

As you can imagine, our family has quite a few recipes that are considered staples. Those we have in a regular rotation, no matter which member of the family is responsible for preparing the meal.

Many of these appear here, exactly as Nani prepares them in her kitchen, while others include tweaks & additions made by members of the family to fit their varying dietary needs or preferences.

If there's one thing Nani believes, it's that there's no right or wrong way to make a meal - what matters is that in the end, it tastes good, leaves you with a full belly, heart, & a smile on your face. That even goes for whoever is left to do the dishes.

every meal is better with a loaf of crusty bread

one of our family's many sacred *sauce* pots

GRAMPIE LUPO'S SPAGHETTI MEAT SAUCE
"THE SAUCE"

This recipe is as old as our family.

'The Sauce' was originally created by Nani's paternal Grandmother, Pasquallela *(Patricia in English)* Scirocco Lupo, who then passed it down to Nani's father, Giovanni Giuseppe *(John Joseph in English)*, one of the last family members to receive a fully Italian name on their birth certificate.

Grandmother Pasquallela was said to have always had a pot of sauce bubbling on the stove & as you walked through the kitchen, it was expected that you'd dip a piece of crusty bread directly into the pot to give it a taste. A tradition we proudly uphold to this day.

Francesco Lupo & Pasquallela (Scirocco) Lupo *(Francis & Patricia)*

When he was old enough, Nani's father (Grampie Lupo) took over the weekly duty of making 'the sauce' & while he followed his mother's recipe for the most part, he set out to make every pot of sauce a little better than the last. This often meant tossing in whatever leftover meat was in the family fridge. A little roasted chicken, braised pork, steak, whatever was on hand went into the pot.

Grampie Lupo could often be heard saying, *'This will be the best sauce yet,'* & it would be... until the next batch.

John & Birtha Lupo, *Grampie & Grammie*

Linda, Barbara, Cathy, Pepe, Meme, Mom, Dad, Judy, Jack & Betsy

'*The sauce*' can be smelled, bubbling away in many of our family kitchens no less than 3 days a week, but especially on Sundays. We all have our own little tweaks we like to make, but the base, the spirit, the foundation of '*the sauce*' always remains the same.

This sauce can be prepared without meat as a vegetarian option, can be used to simmer Nani's Meatballs & is the only sauce to ever fill the 11-layers of our family's famous lasagna.

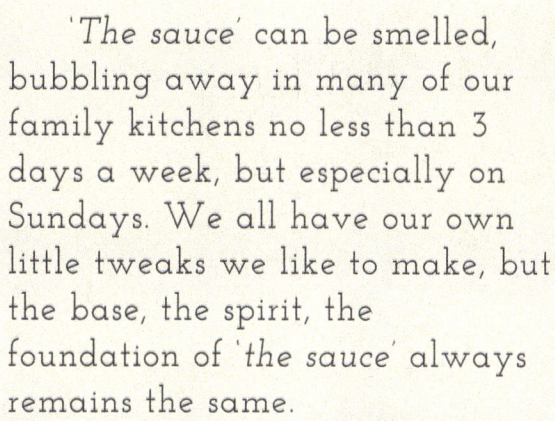

Cornelia Merkelbach Breault, *Meme Breault*

John (back row center) & Birtha Lupo (front row center) with friends

"THE SAUCE"

Ingredients

1 lb ground pork
1 lb ground beef
1 onion, chopped fine
1 green pepper, chopped fine
1-2 cloves garlic, minced fine
2 bay leaves
1 tbsp Italian seasoning
1 tbsp parsley

2 cans plain tomato sauce
1 can tomato paste
1 can diced or stewed tomatoes
1/2 - 1 cup red wine
3/4 cup parmesan or Romano cheese
2-3 tbsp sugar
salt & pepper to taste

Directions:

In a large pot, brown meat with 2 tbsp olive oil.

Add onion, green pepper & minced garlic.

Combine well & allow meat to continue browning.

Add seasonings & cook for 2 additional minutes.

Add tomato sauce, paste, diced or stewed tomatoes & wine.

Allow to simmer for at least 4 hours.

Add cheese & sugar if necessary.

If sauce is too thick, add chicken broth until desired consistency is reached.

Serve over pasta of your choice & enjoy!

NANI'S MEATBALLS

"My parents used to tell me that 'everything' was Nani's meatballs, just so I would eat. I always ate Nani's meatballs." - Stephanie Avron

Ingredients

1 lb ground pork
1 lb ground beef
1 onion, minced very fine
1 green pepper, chopped fine
1 - 2 eggs
1 ½ cups fresh bread crumbs
¾ cup parmesan cheese
1 tbsp Italian seasoning
1 tsp garlic powder
1 tbsp parsley
salt & pepper to taste

Directions:

In a large bowl, mix all ingredients together. Form into 2 inch balls.

In a heavy skillet, fry meatballs in a bit of olive oil to brown.

Add to sauce & simmer for 2 hrs

Keep the Tradition Alive

Continue to pass along the traditions, family recipes & rituals that have importance in your family. By sharing what you've experienced, you ensure that the love & memories within them lives on in each new generation.
    -Nani

GRAMMIE LUPO'S GIAMBOTO

Ingredients

1 lb Italian sausages, cut in 1/2
1 lb chicken thighs, skin removed
2 green peppers, sliced
2 onions, sliced
1 large can of plum or stewed tomatoes
1 can chicken broth.
Italian seasoning, garlic powder, salt & pepper
1 package Cavatelli, cooked to al dente
Optional: 1 small box button mushrooms

Directions:

Preheat oven to 350 degrees.

In a large skillet, brown sausage & chicken, seasoning well.

Move to a large pan, adding peppers, onions, tomatoes & broth, stirring well.

Bake for 1 hour, adding Cavatelli noodles for last 15 minutes.

Serve with Parmesan cheese & crusty bread.

This is a dish that while delicious right out of the oven, tastes even better on days 2 & 3.

HOMEMADE PESTO

Ingredients

2 packed cups fresh basil
3 cloves garlic
¼ cup nuts (pine, almond, or walnuts)
½ cup olive oil
¼ - ½ cup parmesan or romano cheese

Directions:

In a food processor, combine basil, nuts & garlic.

Drizzle in olive oil while processing.

Add cheese & continue processing until fully incorporated.

Cover pesto with a drizzle of olive oil to store in the fridge, or pour into an ice cube tray & freeze in bags for future use.

Nani making meatballs

Nani & Popi

Mark, DeeDee & Chip

GNOCCHI

Ga-noochi as cousin Michelle calls it

Ingredients

2 potatoes
2 cups flour
1 egg

Directions:

Fill a large pot of salted water to a boil

Peel potatoes & add to pot. Cook until tender but still firm. About 15 minutes.

Drain, cool & mash potatoes with a fork or potato masher.

In a large bowl, combine 1 cup of mashed potatoes, flour & egg.

Knead until dough forms a ball.

Roll & shape small portions of the dough at a time into long snakes or ropes.

On a floured surface, cut snakes into half-inch pieces.

Bring large pot of lightly salted water to a boil.

Drop in gnocchi pieces & cook for 3 to 5 minutes or until gnocchi have risen to the top.

Drain & serve with your favorite sauce, or melted butter & chives.

SPAETZLE

A delicious German side dish to enjoy with Goulasch.

Ingredients

1 lb flour
1 tsp salt
4 eggs
⅛ cup milk or water

Directions:

In a bowl, combine all ingredients.

If too thick, add a tbsp more milk/water until smooth.

Fill a large pot with water & 1 tsp salt. Bring to a boil.

Reduce heat to a slow simmer.

Press batter through a colander or Spaetzle maker into the pot of simmering water.

Work in batches, cooking no more than ⅓ of the mixture at a time.

Let cook for 2-3 minutes, until noodles float.

Remove from the pot with a slotted spoon & allow to drain in a separate colander.

Best enjoyed hot with butter, or sautéed in a pan to crispen.

STROMBOLI

Ingredients

1, 1 lb loaf frozen bread dough, thawed
3 tbsp grated Parmesan cheese
2 tbsp vegetable oil
2 eggs, separate yolks & whites
1 tsp dried parsley
1 tsp dried oregano
1/2 tsp garlic powder
1/4 tsp ground black pepper
5 slices pepperoni
5 slices Virginia baked ham
5 slices provolone cheese
2 tsp vegetable oil
1/4 cup green bell pepper, chopped
1/4 cup onion, chopped
1/4 cup fresh mushrooms, sliced
1/4 tsp Italian seasoning
Optional: 1 small container of ricotta cheese, mixed in with seasonings, Parmesan cheese & egg yolks.

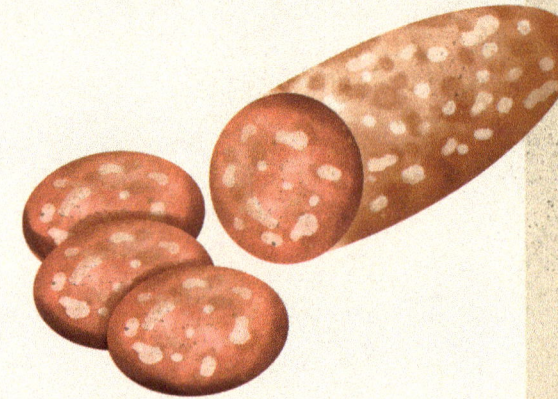

Directions:

Place thawed bread dough in a large bowl in a warm area & let rise until doubled in size, approx. 30 to 60 minutes.

Preheat oven to 350 degrees.

Form dough into a large rectangle on a well-greased baking sheet & set aside.

In a medium bowl, mix 2 tbsp Parmesan cheese, 2 tbsp vegetable oil, egg yolks, parsley, oregano, garlic powder & black pepper.

Spread mixture evenly onto dough.

Layer on top of parmesan mixture, pepperoni, ham & provolone cheese.

In a large skillet over medium heat, sauté 2 tsp vegetable oil, green pepper, onion & mushrooms for 5-10 minutes, until tender.

Spoon vegetables over dough.

Starting at one of the longer sides of your dough, carefully roll until you've formed one large log with all toppings tucked inside.

Place Stromboli seam side down on the baking sheet.

Brush top with egg whites, then sprinkle with 1 tbsp Parmesan cheese & Italian seasoning. Slice top with 5 or 6 diagonal lines to allow steam release.

Bake until golden brown, approx. 30 to 40 minutes.

The Importance of Clean Up

A tidy workspace not only makes cooking easier but also creates a sense of peace & accomplishment. How you leave things whether in the kitchen or in life matters. It doesn't need to be perfect, but it does need to be done.

-Nani

This spoon is over 100 years old. It belonged to!
  Paulina Wettestad

Mother of Gust Wettestad

Grandmother of Martha Avron

It is from Norway. Given to James Avron in 1988, by a cousin.

DILL PICKLES

These can be made into spears, chunks, or whole pickles depending on your family's preference.

Ingredients

6 cups water
½ cup salt
2 cups white vinegar
fresh dill (for top & bottom of each jar)
pickling cucumbers
5 large canning jars

Directions:

Bring to a boil water, salt & vinegar.

Place a few sprigs of fresh dill into the bottom of each jar, then pack full with cucumbers.

Pour hot brine into each jar & top with additional dill.

Seal lids tightly & carefully place each jar into a hot water bath.

Cook until the color of the cucumbers changes then remove from heat & allow the hot water bath to cool.

Carefully remove jars, dry & store in a cool dry place.

TENDERIZING BRINE

For 4lbs of meat; beef, venison, pork, turkey, or chicken.

Marinades can damage the structure of meat, causing it to become mushy. Instead, tenderize your meat with a brine.

Ingredients

1 ½ cups pickling salt
1 ¼ cups sugar
water

Optional: bay leaves, juniper berries, cracked black pepper, chile pepper, thyme, celery seed

Directions:

Fill a large bowl or pan with with enough water so that meat will be covered.

Dissolve pickling salt & sugar in water so it tastes like sweet sea water.

Add any optional flavor enhancers at this time.

Add meat to the brine solution & store in the fridge for ½ hour to 4 hours.

Be sure not to brine your meat for longer than 1 day.

TURKEY & STUFFING MEATLOAF

Ingredients

2 ½ lbs ground turkey
1 ½ cups stuffing mix (chicken flavor)
1 eggs
½ cup celery, diced
½ cup onion, diced
1 clove garlic, minced
⅓ cup milk

Directions:

Preheat oven to 350 degrees.

Combine all ingredients together in a large bowl. *Mixture will be lumpy when combined.*

Spray a 9x5 loaf pan with non-stick cooking spray & fill with mixture.

Bake for 1 hour, until temperature reads 165 degrees at center of loaf.

Serve with mashed potatoes, gravy & steamed veggies.

Serves 6-8.

Learn From the Past

Just as a family recipe improves with each generation, so does the wisdom passed down. Each meal has a story behind it & each ingredient carries a tradition. Learn from the mistakes & successes of those who came before you.
  -Nani

TORTELLINI SOUP

Ingredients

1 package fresh tortellini (*Any fresh tortellini will do, but our family prefers prosciutto & cheese.*)
1 stalk celery, chopped fine
1 small onion, chopped fine
2 tbsp butter
2 tbsp olive oil
1 tbsp dried parsley
pinch of pepper
1 tbsp Italian seasoning
1 box chicken broth/stock

Directions:

Melt butter & oil together in a large pot.

Add celery & onion, cook until translucent & slightly brown along the edges.

Add parsley, pepper & Italian seasoning. Stir.

Cook for 1 minute then add chicken broth/stock & stir.

Bring to a low boil then add tortellini.

Simmer for 4 minutes stirring occasionally.

Serve while hot & top with a sprinkle of fresh parmesan cheese.

GOULASCH

Ingredients

2 lbs stew meat, cut into cubes
3 small onions, chopped (or pureed, for *DeeDee*)
1 can mushrooms
1 can tomato sauce
1-2 tbsp sweet paprika
1-2 tsp minced garlic
2 tbsp olive oil
2 tbsp butter
salt & pepper to taste
Optional: 3 tbsp corn starch & a dollop of sour cream

Directions:

Heat oil & butter in a large skillet.

Add stew meat & brown.

Add onions, stir & cook until translucent.

Add 1 cup water, simmer for 1 ½ hours stirring occasionally & adding water as needed to maintain gravy in pan.

Add mushroom & tomato sauce. Mix well.

If you'd like a thicker gravy/sauce: in a small bowl, mix cornstarch w/ cold water & stir into Goulasch mixture until fully incorporated.

Serve with fresh Spaetzle.

From the very first dinner Judy made in our first home together, she's always set out to sprinkle love into whatever she makes. This is one of the things I cherish most about her. Whether she's spending an entire day preparing a feast for our full extended family, or quickly whipping up a dish for the two of us, Judy can do no wrong in the kitchen. Everything she touches turns out delicious & I know much of that is because of the love & care in each dish.

One thing I know Judy loves more than anything, is to have children in her kitchen. It started when our children were growing up. Judy was so patient & caring as she allowed them to participate in the process by doing little things like scooping & measuring ingredients, stirring 'the sauce' & of course, decorating freshly baked cookies. While there were times when the kitchen would get messy with all her added 'help,' My Judy never minded. She always had a smile on her face & you could hear her laughter echo throughout the house while she supported & encouraged them to try their best.

Now, decades later, I know that Judy loves being able to share those time experiences with our grandchildren & great-grandchildren. Being able to teach & pass down many of the same skills & recipes that she taught our kids so many years ago to these new generations fills her heart. It's something you can see in her smile & the sparkle in her eyes. I'm sure that these moments remind her of the times she spent in her own grandmother's kitchen learning to cook as a young girl.

-Gordon 'Popi' Avron (husband, father, grandfather & great-grandfather)

CROCK POT BEAN SOUP
Also known as 'Soup Beans'

Ingredients

1 lb dried pinto beans, soaked overnight, rinsed & drained
2 strips bacon, chopped & cooked
1 medium-large onion, chopped & cooked until translucent
¾ cup carrots, chopped
2 medium potatoes, chopped
1 quart low sodium chicken broth/stock
½ tsp Odobo Seasoning
¼ tsp garlic powder
1 sazon seasoning packet
¼ tsp oregano
2 pinches pepper
1 can stewed tomatoes, chopped
Optional: ¾ lb boneless ham, cooked & chopped

Directions:

Combine all ingredients in a crock pot & cook on low for 8-10 hours, or high for 3-4 hours.

Serve with homemade cornbread.

When I was a kid, one of my favorite meals was Mom's soup beans over rice.

I always pretended that I was a cowboy out on the open range when I ate them. I would grab my spoon full-fisted like I saw the cowboys do on TV & emulate how they shoveled the beans hungrily into their mouths after a long hard day doing whatever cool things cowboys did.

I've been making Nani's soup beans for my own family now for close to 30+ years & to this day, every time I do, it takes me back to my own childhood.

This recipe is the true epitome of comfort food. The only thing it needs is a big hunk of fresh baked cornbread, a large smear of homemade honey butter & maybe a classic Western movie on TV.

-Mark Avron (son)

Mom has always been the best at improving recipes over time. She's always adding a splash of this or a pinch of that to play with the flavors of our family's favorite meals. When I got married I knew that I wanted to take her Soup Beans recipe with me. The trouble was, I'm much more of a 'precise' cook, so when I called Mom up for the recipe & she told me it called for a 'couple shakes' of seasoning, I needed to know exactly how much that meant. A teaspoon, a half-teaspoon? I've prepared this recipe so many times throughout the years, making my own little tweaks, but no matter what I do, it never measures up to the flavor of Mom's soup beans.

When Mom needed to have surgery & wasn't going to be able to cook for several weeks, Dad took over cooking meals for the two them. As he prepared this recipe with her, he wrote it down on his own recipe card, which I now treasure, along with Mom's. As the strength & flavor of spices have evolved over time, so too has Mom's palate for what pairs best together. Just don't ask her how much to add.

-DeeDee Rice (daughter)

TURKEY CHILI

Ingredients

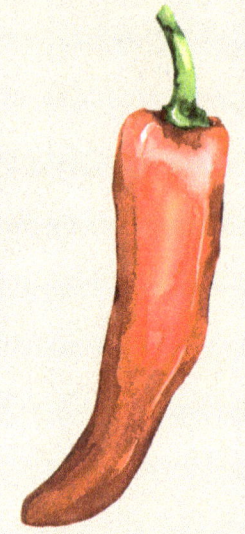

1 1/2 - 2 lbs ground turkey
1 large onion, chopped
1 red or green pepper, chopped
2 tsp adobo seasoning
1 tsp parsley
3 cans beans, drained (pinto, red kidney, black etc)
1 can tomato sauce
1 can diced or stewed tomatoes
1 clove garlic, chopped
¼ tsp garlic powder
1 taco or chili seasoning packet
2 tbsp olive oil
salt & pepper to taste

Directions:

Heat olive oil in a pan.

Add onions, peppers & garlic.

Cook until onions are translucent.

Add ground turkey & cook until done.

Add tomatoes, sauce & seasonings. Stir.

Add beans, cover & simmer for 1-2 hours.

Serve over rice or with homemade cornbread & honey-butter.

Granddaughter Jessica's Variation:

Add: 1 jar of mild mango salsa, an additional red or green pepper (chopped), 2 cups riced cauliflower, 2 tbsp low sodium taco mix, 2 tbsp low sodium chili mix & 1 tsp nutmeg to ingredients above.

Grandson James's Variation:

Add: 2 tbsp low sodium taco mix, 2 tbsp low sodium chili mix, 1/4 cup crispy bacon (chopped fine) & 1 can tomato paste to ingredients above.

My favorite memories with my Nani:

- The smell of Nani's house. It means something yummy is here.
- When Nani plays tea with me. I pour the tea slowly & carefully. You stop when it's at the top.
- Nani's chili & milk with dark cookies. That's my favorite.

-Hayden Greenlow (great-granddaughter)

MINESTRONE SOUP

Ingredients

1 tablespoon olive oil
1 cup onion, diced
3/4 cup carrot, diced
3/4 cup celery, chopped
1 teaspoon garlic, minced
1/2 teaspoons fresh rosemary, minced
1 (15 ounce) can tomato sauce
1 (15 ounce) can cannellini beans, rinsed & drained
2 cups chicken broth
1 cup zucchini, diced
1/2 cup dry Ditalini pasta
1/4 teaspoon black pepper
1/4 cup fresh Italian parsley, chopped
shredded Parmesan cheese (optional)

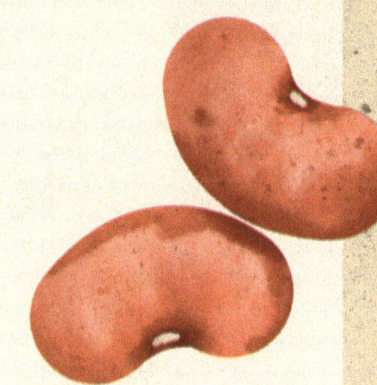

Directions:

Heat olive oil in a large saucepan or Dutch oven over medium-high heat.

Cook onion, carrot, celery, garlic & rosemary until vegetables begin to soften, about 5 minutes.

Stir in tomato sauce, beans, zucchini, pasta, black pepper, broth & 2 1/2 cups water.

Bring to a simmer & cook uncovered, for 10 minutes or until pasta is tender, stirring occasionally.

Serve topped with Parmesan cheese & sprinkle of parsley.

LENTIL SOUP

Ingredients

1 onion, chopped
1/4 cup olive oil
2 carrots, diced
2 stalks celery, chopped
2 cloves garlic, minced
1 teaspoon dried oregano
1 bay leaf
1 teaspoon dried basil
1 (14.5 ounce) can crushed tomatoes
2 cups dry lentils
8 cups water
1/2 cup spinach, rinsed & thinly sliced
salt & pepper to taste

Directions:

In a large soup pot, heat oil over medium heat.

Add onions, carrots & celery; stirring & cooking until onion is tender & translucent.

Add garlic, bay leaf, oregano & basil; cook for 2 minutes.

Stir in lentils, adding water & tomatoes. Bring to a boil.

Reduce heat & simmer for at least 1 hour.

Season to taste with salt & pepper.

When ready to serve, stir in spinach & cook a few moments until it wilts.

Optional: Add a beef bone while cooking for added flavor depth.

LOW-SODIUM CREAM OF CHICKEN SOUP

Ingredients

1 tbsp unsalted butter or olive oil
1 small onion, finely diced
2 tbsp all-purpose flour *(or cornstarch for gluten-free)*
1 cup low-sodium chicken broth
1 cup low-fat or unsweetened milk *(or plant-based alternative)*
1/4 cup cooked shredded chicken *(optional)*
1/4 tsp black pepper
1/4 tsp garlic powder or poultry seasoning

Directions:

In a medium saucepan, heat butter or oil over medium heat.

Add onion & sauté until softened (about 5 minutes).

Sprinkle in flour & stir to coat the onion, cooking for 1-2 minutes.

Slowly whisk in broth, ensuring there are no lumps.

Add milk & seasonings, stirring well.

Simmer & stir until the mixture thickens (about 5-10 minutes).

Remove from heat & blend with an immersion blender or leave chunky, depending on your preference.

Add cooked chicken if desired.

LOW-SODIUM CREAM OF CELERY SOUP

Ingredients

1 tbsp unsalted butter or olive oil
1 small onion, finely diced
2 stalks celery, finely chopped
1 clove garlic, minced
2 tbsp all-purpose flour (or a *gluten-free alternative*)
1 cup low-sodium chicken or vegetable broth
1 cup unsweetened almond milk, low-fat milk, or any preferred milk alternative
1/4 tsp ground black pepper
pinch of herbs like thyme or parsley *(optional)*

Directions:

In a medium saucepan, heat butter or oil over medium heat.

Add onion & celery, cooking until softened (about 5-7 minutes).

Add garlic & cook for 1 minute.

Stir in flour, mixing well to coat vegetable & cook for 1-2 minutes.

Gradually whisk in the broth until smooth.

Add milk & simmer stirring frequently, until it thickens (about 5-10 minutes).

Remove from heat & blend with an immersion blender or leave chunky, depending on your preference.

SPLIT PEA SOUP

Ingredients

1 cup split peas
2 medium sized carrots, chopped
1 ham hock or bone from a ham
½ onion, finely chopped
1 qt water & 1 qt broth
1 small potato, finely diced
salt & pepper to taste

Directions:

Wash peas & cover in water to soak overnight.

In a large pot, bring water, broth & ham hock to a boil for 30 minutes.

Add peas & soaking water to the boiling ham hock.

Boil slowly until peas become mushy, about 1 hour.

Carefully remove ham hock or bone from pot.

Cut any remaining meat from bone may be on bone or ham hock into small pieces & stir back into boiling peas.

Add onion, carrot & potato. Stir well.

Continue to boil slowly until soup has reached your desired consistency.

Add salt & pepper to taste.

Serve & enjoy with crusty bread.

SEAFOOD CHOWDER

Ingredients

2 tbsp butter
3 strips of bacon, cut up into small slices (*Hint: if your bacon is still slightly frozen, use a pair of good kitchen shears.*)
1 lb seafood of your choice (*haddock -cut into small pieces, shrimp, scallops etc.*)
1 small onion, chopped
2-3 stalks of celery, diced
2 medium potatoes, chopped
1 bottle clam juice or broth (*vegetable or chicken*)
1 cup half & half
instant potatoes (*to thicken broth*)
salt, pepper & parsley to taste

Directions:

In a large pan on stove, melt butter & begin frying bacon.

Add onion & celery, cook for 10 minutes.

Stir in potatoes & clam juice or broth & cook another 10 minutes.

Add seafood, cover & simmer until fully cooked.

Add half & half, bring chowder back to simmer & stir in small amounts of instant potatoes at a time. Stopping when you've reached your desired thickness.

Season with salt, pepper & parsley to taste.

Serve with crusty bread & enjoy.

Exploring Italy in style

MACARONI AND CHEESE

Ingredients

1 lb elbow or other tubular pasta, cooked to al dente
6 tbsp unsalted butter
4 tbsp unsalted butter, melted
1 ½ cups panko bread crumbs or any bread crumbs
½ cup flour
3 cups whole milk
¼ tsp smoked paprika
1 cup heavy whipping cream
4 cups sharp cheddar shredded (**not** *the bagged kind*)
2 cups Swiss, smoked Gouda, or Gruyere Cheese, shredded
salt & pepper to taste

Directions:

Preheat oven to 350 degrees.

In large bowl mix 4 tbsp melted butter, bread crumbs & paprika. Set aside.

In a large pot, melt remaining 6 tbsp butter.

Add flour, stirring well & cooking for 2 minutes until fully combined.

Add milk & cream, cooking for 2 minutes.

Add cheese, stirring until fully melted & a creamy sauce forms.

Pour pasta into a large buttered casserole dish, covering with cheese sauce & mixing well without mashing the pasta.

Sprinkle with topping & bake until lightly browned & sauce is bubbling.

MEXICAN PINWHEELS

Ingredients

2 cans refrigerator croissants
1 can bean dip
1 red pepper, chopped
1 green pepper, chopped
1 package shredded cheese
1 small can sliced black or green olives
¼ cup corn meal
salsa & sour cream

Directions:

Preheat oven based on instructions on croissant can

Lightly cover your rolling surface with cornmeal.

Roll out both cans of croissants into a single large rectangle.

Evenly spread bean dip over dough.

Sprinkle with chopped peppers, olives & cheese.

Carefully roll dough into a log, longways like a savory jelly roll.

Cut log into ¾ inch slices & place on a greased cookie sheet.

Bake for 15-20 minutes or until nicely browned & cheese is bubbling.

Enjoy with sour cream & salsa for dipping.

SHEPHERD'S PIE

Ingredients

6 potatoes, mashed with butter & cream
2 cans of vegetables (corn, peas, beans, carrots, etc)
2 lbs ground meat (ground beef, pork, turkey, chicken, venison or a combo)
1 onion, minced
German Jaeger sauce mix
1 cup broth (chicken, beef or vegetable)
salt & pepper to taste
dash of paprika & a bit of butter
Optional: Replace German Jaeger sauce mix & broth with 1 can of brown gravy or cream of mushroom soup.

Nani's granddaughter Jessi likes to use ground turkey, 1 cup cottage cheese & 1-2 cups blended cauliflower for added nutrition.

Directions:

Preheat oven to 400 degrees.

In a large pan, cook meat & onion, until browned.

In a separate smaller pan, make gravy with German Jaeger sauce mix, broth & a dash of paprika.

Simmer for 10 minutes.

Add gravy to meat mixture & combine.

Butter the bottom & sides of a large baking dish.

Layer baking dish with meat & gravy mixture, then vegetables & top with mashed potatoes. Dot the top with butter & a sprinkle of paprika.

Bake for 20 minutes, or until top has started to brown.

Allow to rest for 10 minutes before serving.

Embrace the Mess

The kitchen can get messy & that's okay. Flour on your clothes, spilled sugar, or overturned bowls are all part of the fun. Sometimes life gets messy, too. It's not that serious & that's often when the best memories are made.
   —Nani

NICK'S FAVORITE TUNA CASSEROLE

Ingredients

1 lb egg noodles, cooked as directed
1 cup shredded cheese
2 cans white albacore tuna *(in water)*
1 can cream of mushroom, celery, or chicken soup
1 cup milk or cream
2 cups bread crumbs
4 tbsp melted butter
salt & pepper to taste

Optional: for a healthier low sodium option, you can make your own cream or celery or cream of chicken soup from scratch. Recipes on the following pages.

Directions:

Preheat oven to 350 degrees.

In a large pot, mix soup & milk until bubbly.

Add cheese & tuna, mix well.

In a large casserole dish, combine noodles & tuna mixture.

In a small bowl, combine melted butter, bread crumbs & cheese.

Sprinkle topping on casserole & bake for 20-30 minutes.

Nani's Tuna Casserole makes me feel like I'm 8 years old again. It reminds me of sitting at the dinner table all together as a family, at 6pm every night; each of us had our regular seat at the table.

This recipe reminds me of home in Little Tooky. No matter where I go in life, I'll always have that.

—Nick Rice (grandson)

A Little Bit of Sweetness Goes a Long Way

Whether it's a drizzle of honey in a cup of tea or a dusting of powdered sugar on hot French Toast, a little sweetness can brighten someone's day. This lesson encourages kindness, generosity & finding ways to bring light & joy into each other's lives.
—Nani

BAKED HAM

Ingredients

3-5 lb ham
1/2 stick butter, melted
1/2 cup brown sugar
1 tsp ground mustard

Directions:

Preheat oven to 350 degrees.

In a small saucepan combine butter, brown sugar & mustard, cook for 2 minutes stirring well to keep sugar from burning.

Place ham into a large baking dish & brush liberally with glaze.

Roast for approx. 15 minutes per pound until inside of ham reaches 160 degrees.

Serve & enjoy with sides of baked beans, sweet potatoes, coleslaw & cornbread.

Generosity in Every Serving

Sharing food is an act of love. Whether it's inviting someone to dinner, handing out a plate of leftovers, or a cookie tray at Christmas, generosity comes in many forms & is always appreciated.
   -Nani

MARY'S INSTANT POTATO LEFSE

Ingredients

3 cups instant potato flakes or buds
2 cups boiling water
½ cup milk
½ cup half & half
2 tsp sugar
2 tbsp butter
salt to taste
1 - 1 ½ cups flour

Directions:

In a large pot, combine water, milk, half & half & butter to a boil.

Add potatoes, sugar & salt. Stir well to fully combine.

Remove from heat & use a mixer to blend well.

Cover with paper towels & plastic wrap. Cool thoroughly overnight.

Add flour & mix thoroughly.

Form patties & chill again.

Heat lefse griddle to 400 degrees.

Roll thin & bake until crisp on both sides.

PORK CHOPS

Ingredients

3-4, 6oz pork chops
½ onion, sliced
olive oil or butter
beef broth (amount will vary)
salt & pepper to taste

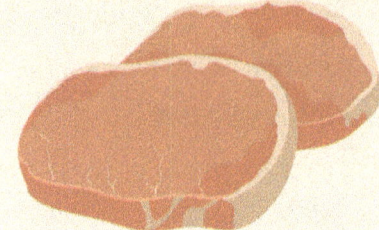

Gravy:
1 tbsp Maggi Jager Sauce
½ cup milk or heavy cream

Directions:

Heat a large skillet or pan over medium heat.

Add oil or butter & onions, cooking for a few minutes until onions are translucent.

With your spatula or spoon, move onions to the outer sides of the skillet & arrange pork chops in center.

Season chops with pepper & brown on both sides, approx. 2-3 minutes each side for thin chops, or 5-6 minutes each side for thicker cuts.

Spoon cooked onions over the top of pork chops & pour broth into skillet until the chops are 75% covered.

Cover & simmer on low heat for 45 minutes. Check broth level frequently to ensure chops remain partially submerged, adding more broth as needed.

After 45 minutes, check meat with a fork. It's done when it begins to fall off the bone easily.

If necessary, continue cooking in 30 minute increments until meat is done.

Once pork chops are finished, carefully remove chops & onions from skillet.

Into pan dripping add Maggi Jager Sauce & milk. Stir well until fully combined.

Serve & enjoy!

When I was just a little kid, I remember running into Nani & Popi's house for the first time & being greeted with a big hug. That's what I feel when I think of Little Tooky. The dirt road that leads everyone to a place where they feel welcome & included. Little Tooky is a place of gathering.

Throughout my childhood & adolescence, during the winter school break, my family would make the 6-hour drive up to New Hampshire from New Jersey. Over the holidays one of the most important things we did was make lefse. I remember Nani & other family members educating us on Popi's upbringing. How lefse is a Norwegian tradition & both Nani & Popi had made it with the pros.

In our family, cooking isn't just something we do for survival, it's something you do when family comes to visit. It's something you do every Sunday when your children & grandchildren come for dinner. Food is a love language in Nani & Popi's house, it's a way of connecting, loving & enjoying each other. That's something Nani has instilled in each of us.

-Laura Leggiero (granddaughter)

MASHED SWEET POTATOES

Ingredients

5-6 large sweet potatoes, raw
⅓ cup milk, room temperature
2-3 tbsp butter, softened
½ tsp cinnamon

Optional:
2 tbsp pure maple syrup
½ cup mini marshmallows
¼ cup pecans, chopped

Directions:

In a large pot, cover potatoes (with skins on) with water & boil for 15-20 minutes.

Drain & carefully peel skins from potatoes while hot. (Using a potholder to hold onto the hot potatoes can help.)

In a large bowl, combine potatoes, milk, butter & cinnamon.

Mix well with a mixer or masher.

These can be served as is at this point. However, Nani likes to do a little more.

Set oven to broil.

Pour potato mixture into a deep oven-safe dish & top with sprinkled marshmallows & pecans. Broil potatoes, watching closely, only until the marshmallows have started to turn golden brown. Carefully remove from the oven & enjoy.

SALMON PATTIES

Ingredients

2 cans salmon, drained
¼ ream saltine crackers, crushed well, or ½ cup bread crumbs
1 egg
1 large sweet potato, boiled & mashed
1 tsp parsley
½ tsp garlic, minced
1 tbsp lemon juice
½ cup onion, chopped
½ red pepper, chopped

For frying:
¼ cup soybean oil
2 tbsp butter

Directions:

In a large bowl combine all ingredients.

Form into patties (makes approx. 10-12 patties).

In a medium-sized pan, heat oil & butter.

Fry patties 1-2 at a time. Be careful not to overcrowd the pan.

When browned on both sides, move to a baking sheet or plate, covered with a paper towel to absorb excess oil

Enjoy with homemade tarter sauce & coleslaw, or apple sauce

HADDOCK AU GRATIN

Ingredients

2-3 large pieces of haddock (or other white fish)
2 medium potatoes
1 medium onion, sliced
3/4 -1 cup half & half or milk
3/4 cup frozen green peas
5 tbsp butter
parsley
salt & pepper to taste

Directions:

Preheat oven to 350 degrees.

Place potatoes in a medium pot, fill with water & bring to a boil.

Cook for 5 minutes, drain & set aside to cool slightly.

Butter the bottom & sides of a deep baking dish.

Arrange fish in the bottom of the pan.

Sprinkle fish with salt, pepper & parsley.

Cut potatoes into thin slices.

Dot fish pieces with butter, then layer with potatoes, onions & peas.

Pour half & half or milk over top, cover with aluminum foil & bake for 20-25 minutes.

OVEN BAKED FISH

Ingredients

2-3 large filets of your favorite white fish (Haddock, Cod, or Halibut)
5 tbsp butter, melted
½ cup breadcrumbs
parsley
salt & pepper to taste

Directions:

Preheat oven to 350 degrees.

In a medium bowl, combine breadcrumbs & parsley.

Sprinkle filets with salt & pepper.

Dip filets into melted butter, then breadcrumbs & place in the bottom of a large baking dish.

Place a small dab of butter on top of each filet.

Bake for 15-20 minutes max.

Serve with a slice of fresh lemon, a sprinkle of dill & homemade tarter sauce for dipping.

Don't Be Afraid to Experiment

Even the most traditional recipes can be made new with a little creativity. Don't be afraid to try new things & embrace change in both cooking & life.
    -Nani

PAN SEARED SALMON

Ingredients

3-4 large filets of salmon
2 tbsp butter
vegetable or olive oil
Old Bay seasoning
salt & pepper to taste

Directions:

Lightly season both sides of the filets with salt, pepper & Old Bay Seasoning.

Heat a large pan on the stove until very hot. *(Our family loves to use a cast iron pan for this.)*

Add a splash of oil & butter to the pan.

Place filets (the number will vary on the size of your pan) skin side down into the pan & allow to sear for 6-8 minutes.

Carefully flip filets & remove the skin while the second side sears for 2 minutes.

If necessary, add a bit more butter to the pan & flip the filets again, to re-sear the side where skin has been removed.

Serve with your favorite vegetables & rice pilaf.

SWEET CORNBREAD

Ingredients

1 cup all purpose flour
1 cup yellow corn meal
2/3 cups sugar
3 1/2 tsp baking powder
1 tsp salt
1 cup milk
1/3 cup vegetable oil
1 egg

Directions:

Preheat oven to 400°.

Grease bottom & sides of an 8-9 inch pan & place into oven to warm. (*Our family likes to use a cast iron pan for added flavor.*)

In a large bowl, combine all dry ingredients.

Add wet ingredients & mix until fully combined.

Carefully remove pan from the oven & fill with batter. (*This should sizzle.*)

Bake 20-25 minutes until light golden brown & a toothpick inserted into the center comes out clean.

Enjoy while warm with butter, honey, or plain.

Serves approx. 9 people.

Nani, Popi, Mark, Chip & DeeDee

Nani & Hunter

SNICKERDOODLES

Ingredients

1 cup shortening
1 ½ cups sugar
2 eggs
2 ¾ cups flour
2 tsp cream of tartar
1 tsp baking soda
¼ tsp salt

Rolling Mixture:
2 tbsp sugar
2 tsp cinnamon

Directions:

Preheat oven to 400 degrees.

Mix together shortening, 1 ½ cups sugar & eggs.

In a separate bowl blend together dry ingredients.

Combine & shape dough into 1-inch balls.

Roll each ball in a mixture of sugar & cinnamon.

Place balls 2 inches apart on an ungreased baking sheet.

Bake for 8 to 10 minutes. Cookies will puff up at first but then flatten & crack slightly.

Makes approx 6 dozen cookies

BANANA BREAD

Ingredients

1 ¾ cup flour
2 tsp baking powder
¼ tsp baking soda
¼ tsp salt
⅓ cup shortening
⅔ cup sugar
2 eggs
1 cup bananas, smashes (approx 2)
½ cup nuts, chopped

Directions:

Preheat oven to 350 degrees.

Grease the bottom & sides of a loaf pan & set aside.

In a large bowl, sift together all dry ingredients.

In a separate bowl, cream together shortening & sugar.

Add eggs & banana to bowl with sugar & combine.

Pour the wet mixture into the dry & stir well.

Add nuts & stir. Do not beat or over-mix.

Move batter into greased loaf pan & bake for 40-50 minutes.

Allow to cool before slicing. Enjoy warm with butter or peanut butter.

ZUCCHINI BREAD

Ingredients

3/4 cup salad oil
1 1/2 cups sugar
3 eggs, well beaten
2 1/2 cups zucchini, shredded
1/2 cup applesauce
3 tsp vanilla extract
zest of 1 orange
3 cups flour
1 tsp baking powder
1 tsp baking soda
1 tsp salt
3 tsp cinnamon
1/2 tsp nutmeg

Topping:
2 tbsp cinnamon
4 tbsp sugar

Directions:

Preheat oven to 350 degrees & grease the bottom & sides of 2 loaf pans.

In a large bowl, mix together salad oil, sugar, eggs, zucchini, applesauce, vanilla & orange zest. Set aside.

In a separate bowl, combine flour, baking powder, baking soda, salt, cinnamon & nutmeg.

Add wet ingredients to dry ingredients & mix well.

Pour batter evenly into 2 loaf pans & sprinkle tops with cinnamon sugar mixture.

Bake for 45 minutes, then reduce heat to 325 degrees & bake for an additional 30 minutes.

Remove from oven & cool on wire rack.

Enjoy while still warm with butter or store in an airtight container.

For as long as I can remember I've been baking next to my mom & my grandmother. One of my fondest memories though is from when I was about 8. I was finally old enough to be able to follow along with a recipe on my own & the one I enjoyed making the most was Nani's Zucchini Bread.

I entered Nani's Zucchini Bread recipe into the Hopkinton State Fair for four years starting at age 8. Nani taught me that it wasn't just about what went into the bread but also about presentation. We wrapped the loaf in a beautiful cloth, sat it in a basket & added a small jar of butter with a knife for spreading.

At the time, I was beyond excited about the Blue Ribbon I received year after year & kept them displayed proudly in my room. Now, as an adult, I know that those ribbons were as much hers as they were mine & in reality, I won an even bigger prize just by having my Nani as a constant loving & supportive presence in my life.

-Jessica Greenlow (granddaughter)

BLACKBERRY MUFFINS

Ingredients

2 cups flour
1 tbsp baking powder
¼ tsp salt
1 egg
½ cup brown sugar, packed
¼ cup sugar
½ cup fat-free sour cream
¾ cup buttermilk
4 tbsp butter, melted & cooled
1 ½ cups fresh blackberries, washed

Directions:

Preheat oven to 350 degrees & generously grease a standard muffin tin.

In a large mixing bowl, whisk together flour, baking powder & salt.

In a separate bowl, beat the egg.

Whisk in sugar & sour cream until mixture is fully combined.

Add buttermilk & melted butter.

Carefully sprinkle blackberries into the bowl with dry ingredients then slowly add the wet mixture & fold to combine.

Be careful not to over mix.

Divide batter into greased muffin tin with a large spoon or ice cream scoop & bake until a toothpick inserted into the center of the muffins comes out clean. approx. 20-25 minutes.

Remove from the pan & cool on a rack.

Enjoy while still warm with butter.

The first time I can remember Nani making Blackberry Muffins was in 1970, while our family was living in San Francisco, California. I was probably about 11 years old & my brother, sister & I would run to pick blackberries from the bushes that grew in the woods behind our house. As soon as they were in season, we would carry our buckets & bowls into the trees & pick a whole mess of the sweet berries. We would snack as we picked & I'm surprised we didn't make ourselves sick. I remember trying my best to keep from eating too many berries fresh, so I could bring enough home for Mom. She baked blackberry everything, but my favorite was these delicious Blackberry Muffins.

There's nothing better than seeing the fruits of your labor turned into a warmed baked pastry, enjoyed straight out of the oven & slathered with butter. To this day, anytime I enjoy a blackberry muffin, it brings me back to those moments; those incredible memories of Nani & the ways she can transform something as simple as blackberries into a magical treat.

-Mark Avron (son)

HAZELNUT CAKE

Ingredients

1 ½ cup flour
2 tsp baking powder
¼ tsp salt
½ cup butter, melted
¼ cup oil
1 cup sugar
2 eggs, separated
1 tsp vanilla extract
½ cup milk
1 cup chopped nuts
¼ cup sour cream

Maple Topping:
1 ½ cup brown sugar
¾ cup maple syrup
6 tbsp butter

Directions:

Preheat oven to 350 degrees. Grease the bottom & sides of a 9x13-inch baking dish.

In a small bowl, beat egg whites until frothy & set aside.

In a large bowl, mix together butter & oil.

Add sugar & stir well.

Add egg yolks, vanilla & milk. Mix until combined.

Sift flour, baking powder & salt into the bowl, stirring to combine.

Add nuts & sour cream. Stir well.

Carefully fold in beaten egg whites.

Pour into the greased dish & bake for 50 minutes.

Remove from oven & allow to cool in the pan.

In a small saucepan bring Maple Topping ingredients to a boil.

Cook for 3 minutes stirring constantly.

Remove cake from pan & set on a clean plate or serving dish.

Carefully drizzle topping across over the cake.

Trust Your Instincts

Not every recipe comes with perfect measurements & sometimes you have to trust your intuition. This lesson extends to every part of life, trust your instincts & don't be afraid to make decisions on your own.
   -Nani

BETTER THAN ROBERT REDFORD

Ingredients

1 cup flour
1 cup walnuts or pecans, coarsely chopped
1 stick unsalted butter, melted
1 x 8-ounce) package cream cheese, softened
1 cup confectioners sugar
1 x 8-ounce) container frozen whipped topping
4 cups milk
2 x 3 ½-ounce boxes instant vanilla pudding
2 x 4-ounce boxes instant chocolate pudding mix
chopped nuts
chocolate curls or shavings

Directions:

Preheat oven to 350 degrees.

Coat a 9 x 13 x 2-inch baking dish with nonstick cooking spray.

In a medium bowl, mix flour, nuts & butter.

Pat firmly into the bottom of prepared dish.

Bake for 15 minutes.

Remove from oven & allow to cool.

In another bowl, beat cream cheese & sugar until smooth.

Fold half of the whipped topping into the bowl.

Spread over cooled crust.

Prepare vanilla pudding using 2 cups of the milk.

Spread into the pan.

Prepare chocolate pudding with the remaining 2 cups of milk.

Spread into the pan.

Spread the remaining whipped topping into the pan.

Refrigerate for at least 2 hours.

Sprinkle with additional chopped nuts & chocolate before serving.

I don't necessarily love the name so much, but Nani's 'Better Than Robert Redford' dessert is so delicious, it doesn't even matter. I don't know what I love most, the walnut crust, the chocolate pudding, the cheesecake, or the whipped cream. I've been eating this dessert for over 40 years & every time she makes it tastes better than the last. I think I might love the cheese cake filling best- but I might have to try it again just to make sure.

There's really isn't anything Nani can't do or make in the kitchen.

-Chuck Rice (son-in-law)

VIKING COFFEE

Ingredients

1 oz Kamora Coffee Liqueur
1 oz Kahlua
1 oz Baileys Irish Cream
hot strong coffee
whipped cream
cinnamon or nutmeg

Directions:

Combine coffee, liqueur, Kahlua & Irish Cream in a mug to your taste preference.

Top with a large dollop of whipped cream & a sprinkle of cinnamon or nutmeg.

Enjoy responsibly.

Never Skip the Tasting

Taste as you go. Not just in cooking, but in life. Take time to savor the moments, enjoy the journey & adjust as needed. The best results come when you take the time to check in & give thanks along the way.

—Nani

NANI'S GENERAL COOKING TERMS & DEFINITIONS

Included here is a detailed glossary of cooking terms for everyday cooks to learn & use confidently in the kitchen.

A

- **Al Dente:** Italian for "to the tooth," referring to pasta, rice, or vegetables cooked until tender but firm to the bite.
- **Au Jus:** French for "with juice," meaning serving meat with its natural juices.
- **Aerate:** (Air-er-ate) To add air into a mixture, such as by sifting flour or whisking egg whites.

B

- **Bake:** To cook food in an oven with dry heat, like bread or cakes.
- **Baste:** To brush or spoon liquids over food while it cooks to keep it moist & add flavor.
- **Blanch:** To briefly cook food in boiling water, typically vegetables or fruits, then quickly cooled in ice water. This can, preserve color & texture, Loosens outer skins of produce for easy peeling, Stop Enzyme Action, Prevents spoilage & helps retain quality for freezing. Pre-cooking: Softens food slightly for further cooking methods like sautéing, stir-frying, or roasting.
- **Boil:** To heat a liquid until it reaches 212°F (100°C) & bubbles vigorously.
- **Braise:** To brown food first, then cook it slowly in a small amount of liquid in a covered pot.
- **Bread:** To coat food in breadcrumbs or a dry mixture before frying or baking for a crispy texture.
- **Broil:** To cook food under direct high heat, usually in an oven. "Keep your eye on it! Broiling cooks fast & you can burn it before you know it."
- **Brown:** To cook food over medium or high heat with an oil or butter until it turns golden or dark brown for flavor development. This is not frying.

C

- **Caramelize:** To cook sugar or foods with natural sugars until golden or brown, enhancing sweetness.
- **Chop:** To cut food into small, uneven pieces.
- **Cream:** To beat butter & sugar until fluffy, often for baking.
- **Crudités:** A platter of raw vegetables served with a dipping sauce.
- **Cube:** To cut food into uniform square pieces, typically 1/2 inch or larger.
- **Curdle:** When a liquid separates into solid curds & liquid whey, often due to heat or acid.
- **Cut In:** To combine fat (like butter) into flour using a pastry cutter, fork, or fingers, creating a crumbly texture.

D

- **Debone:** To remove bones from meat, poultry, or fish.
- **Deglaze:** To add liquid to a hot pan to dissolve & loosen browned bits for a flavorful sauce.
- **Degrease:** To skim fat from the surface of a liquid, like broth or sauce.
- **Deep-Fat Fry:** To fully submerge food in hot oil, creating a crispy exterior.
- **Dice:** To cut food into small, uniform cubes, typically 1/4 to 1/2 inch.
- **Dredge:** To coat food lightly in flour, breadcrumbs, or another dry ingredient before cooking.
- **Drippings:** Fat & juices released during cooking meat, often used for making gravy.
- **Dry Marinade:** A mixture of dry herbs & spices rubbed onto food for flavor before cooking.

E

- **Egg Wash**: Beaten egg (with or without milk or water) brushed on baked goods for a shiny finish.
- **Emulsify**: To mix two liquids, like oil & vinegar, into a smooth mixture.

F

- **Fillet:** A boneless piece of meat or fish, or the process of removing bones.
- **Fines Herbs:** A mix of fresh, finely chopped herbs like parsley, chives, tarragon & chervil.
- **Flambé:** To ignite alcohol in a dish to burn off alcohol & enhance flavor.
- **Flake:** To gently break cooked food, like fish, into small pieces.
- **Fold:** To incorporate (combine ingredients) a delicate substance, such as whipped cream or beaten egg whites, into another substance without releasing air bubbles. A spatula is used to gently bring part of the mixture from the bottom of the bowl to the top; the process is repeated, while slowly rotating the bowl, until the ingredients are thoroughly blended.
- **Fricassee:** To lightly sauté meat & then simmer it in a sauce or broth.
- **Fry:** To cook food in hot oil or fat, either shallow or deep.

G

- **Glaze:** A shiny coating applied to food, like icing or a sauce.
- **Grate:** To shred food into small pieces using a grater.
- **Grill:** To cook food over direct heat, usually on a barbecue or grill pan.

H

- **Hollandaise:** A rich sauce made with butter, egg yolks & lemon juice or vinegar.
- **Hull:** To remove the leafy tops of strawberries or the outer covering of seeds.

I

- **Ice Bath:** A bowl of ice & water used to quickly cool food.
- **Incorporate:** To blend ingredients together until they are fully combined, creating a uniform mixture. This can be done by stirring, folding, or mixing, depending on the recipe.
- **Infuse:** To steep ingredients in liquid to release their flavors.

J
- **Julienne:** To cut food into thin, matchstick-sized strips.

K
- **Knead:** To work dough by hand or machine to make it smooth & elastic.

L
- **Lard:** To insert strips of fat into meat for moisture during cooking.
- **Leavening:** Ingredients like yeast or baking powder that cause dough to rise.

M
- **Macerate:** To soak food, typically fruit, in liquid to soften & flavor it.
- **Marinade:** A seasoned liquid for soaking food before cooking to enhance flavor.
- **Marinate:** The process of soaking food in a marinade.
- **Meunière:** A preparation of fish dredged in flour, sautéed in butter & served with lemon-butter sauce.
- **Mince:** To chop food into very fine, small pieces.

P
- **Pan Fry:** To cook food in hot oil or fat, usually over direct heat. The food is not stirred, but is simply cooked on one or both sides. (see Deep-fat fry, Stir-Fry, Saute).
- **Parboil:** To partially cook food in boiling water before finishing with another method.
- **Pare:** To remove the skin or peel from fruits & vegetables.
- **Plump:** To soak dried food, like raisins, in liquid to restore moisture.
- **Poach:** To gently cook food in simmering liquid.
- **Purée:** To blend food into a smooth, thick paste.

R

- **Reduce:** To simmer a liquid to evaporate water & concentrate flavor.
- **Refresh:** To cool hot food quickly in cold water or an ice bath.
- **Render:** To melt solid fat into liquid by slow heating.
- **Roast:** To cook food in an oven or over an open flame using dry heat. This method often involves browning the outside of the food to develop flavor while maintaining tenderness inside, commonly used for meats, vegetables & nuts.
- **Roux:** A cooked mixture of fat & flour used to thicken sauces & soups.

S

- **Sauté:** To cook food quickly in a small amount of oil or butter.
- **Scald:** To heat liquid until just before boiling or to loosen skins.
- **Score:** To make shallow cuts on the surface of food for even cooking or flavor absorption.
- **Sear:** To brown food over high heat, forming a flavorful crust.
- **"Shaking hands with herbs":** rub the herbs together in your hands until you can smell the fragrance.
- **Simmer:** To cook gently in liquid just below boiling, usually for a long period of time.
- **Sliver:** To cut into long thin pieces. See also julienne.
- **Steam:** To cook food using the steam from boiling water.
- **Steep:** To soak food, like tea or herbs, in hot liquid to release flavor.
- **Stir Fry:** A Chinese method of preparing meat or vegetables by cooking very rapidly in a frying pan or wok over high heat, stirring constantly.
- **Supreme:** To remove the membrane from citrus segments.

T

- **Temper:** To mix hot liquid slowly into a cold ingredient to prevent curdling.
- **Tenderize:** To make meat softer by pounding or marinating.
- **Toast:** To brown food using dry heat.
- **Toss:** To mix ingredients lightly, like salad.
- **Truss:** To tie meat, like poultry, with string for even cooking.

U
- **Umami:** A savory, rich flavor found in foods like mushrooms & soy sauce.

V
- **Vinaigrette:** A dressing made of oil, vinegar & seasonings.

W
- **Whisk:** To mix ingredients quickly with a whisk.
- **Whip:** To beat cream or eggs to add air, making them fluffy.

Z
- **Zest:** The outer peel of citrus fruits used for flavor, usually grated.

You Don't Need to Follow the Recipe Exactly

Life rarely goes according to plan & that's okay. Sometimes the best things happen when you break the rules, add your own touch & trust that you'll be just fine without a strict blueprint. When you choose your own path, you get to have an adventure.

—Nani

SUPPORTIVE SIDES & SERVING SUGGESTIONS

Recipe	Suggested Sides/Additions	Benefits
Grampie Lupo's Spaghetti Meat Sauce	Mixed greens salad with vinaigrette; garlic bread; steamed broccoli or roasted vegetables	Provides fiber, vitamins (A, C, K) & healthy fats; compliments the meal's protein & carbs.
Lasagna	Steamed green beans or zucchini; arugula salad with lemon dressing; whole-grain bread	Balances rich cheese & pasta with light veggies; adds fiber, magnesium, & additional antioxidants.
Macaroni & Cheese	Steamed spinach or kale; roasted Brussels sprouts; grilled chicken breast or turkey slices	Adds protein, leafy greens for calcium & iron, & reduces the meal's high carb & fat concentration.
Gnocchi	Tomato & cucumber salad; sautéed mushrooms & spinach; grilled shrimp or salmon	Adds omega-3s, antioxidants & fiber; balances the starchy nature of gnocchi.
Meatballs (Italian)	Roasted cauliflower or eggplant; whole-grain bread; a fresh tomato & basil salad	Adds fiber, phytonutrients & healthier carb options while lightening the meat-heavy dish.
Schnitzel	German potato salad (with vinegar, not mayo); sautéed red cabbage; steamed asparagus	Balances fried pork with fiber, vitamins & a tangy counterbalance to the rich schnitzel.
Charcuterie Board	Fresh fruit like grapes, berries, or melon; raw vegetables with hummus; whole-grain crackers	Adds fiber, vitamins & whole grains to complement the rich meats & cheeses.

Shepherd's Pie	fresh mixed greens with lemon dressing; whole-grain roll	Increases vitamin A & fiber; adds a refreshing contrast to the rich meat & potato pie.
Italian Baked Stew	Roasted sweet potatoes; sautéed spinach & garlic; a small side of whole-grain pasta	Adds complex carbs & iron; complements the hearty chicken & sausage dish.
Tuna Casserole	Steamed broccoli or green beans; roasted cherry tomatoes; a side of quinoa or brown rice; greens with mixed veggies	Enhances the meal's omega-3s & adds more whole-grain fiber to complement the casserole.
Ham Supper	Roasted Brussels sprouts or carrots; quinoa salad with cranberries & almonds; apple slices	Balances the richness of ham with light, fiber-rich veggies & fruits & provides healthy fats.
Stromboli	Arugula & parmesan salad; roasted bell peppers & zucchini; marinara dipping sauce	Adds fiber & vitamins, balances the carb-heavy dish & offers a lighter option alongside Stromboli.
Mexican Pinwheels	Black bean & corn salad; avocado slices or guacamole; a side of roasted sweet potato fries	Adds fiber, healthy fats & a variety of nutrients to complement the cheesy pinwheels.
Sweet Corn Bread	Chili or vegetable soup; roasted root vegetables; side of black-eyed peas or a bean salad	Balances sweetness with hearty & nutrient-rich pairings like beans & vegetables.

Apple Pie	Vanilla Greek yogurt or whipped coconut cream; sliced almonds or walnuts; a side of fresh fruit salad, or a scoop of vanilla Ice cream.	Provides protein, healthy fats & light, refreshing elements to balance the sweetness of the pie.
Lentil Soup	Whole-grain bread or pita; a side of roasted cauliflower or green beans; small side salad with vinaigrette	Enhances fiber & protein; offers textural contrast & a refreshing addition to the hearty soup.
Minestrone Soup	Whole-grain crackers; grilled chicken breast or fish; a fresh side of kale chips or roasted veggies	Adds protein & complements the nutrient-rich veggie soup with light, healthy sides.
Seafood Chowder	A small spinach & strawberry salad; whole-grain bread or crackers; roasted asparagus	Balances the richness with antioxidants, fiber & omega-3s.
Split Pea Soup	Whole-grain toast with avocado; a side of sautéed greens; roasted root vegetables	Complements protein-rich soup with healthy fats, iron & vitamins.
Tortellini en Brodo	Steamed green beans; roasted cherry tomatoes; a light mixed greens salad	Adds fiber, vitamins & a fresh balance to the hearty broth & pasta.
Chili	Cornbread or whole-grain rolls; side of coleslaw or fresh corn salad; sliced avocado	Adds fiber, healthy fats & crunch to balance the rich, spicy chili.

SEASONAL FRESH VEGETABLE & FRUITS BUYING GUIDE

Nani always tells us, "Use your common sense. You're going to buy seasonally fresh things because they're the freshest & best value. If something is out of season, you'll typically pay more for it & it's not going to be as good. The very best things will always come from your own garden. You'll know what's gone into your soil, what you put into the plants & how long it's been since you last harvested. The next best thing is to shop at local open markets. Somewhere over the years, this seems to have been lost, or not as accessible as it used to be. At the end of the day, though, something is always better than nothing & you can't be afraid of using canned or frozen things. It just doesn't need to be that complicated."

This is Nani's guide & should help you choose the best fresh produce each season to enjoy peak flavor, nutrition & value. Remember that exact availability may vary by region.

Spring (March - May)

Fruits:
- Strawberries: Sweet and juicy, look for bright red berries with no green or white shoulders.
- Pineapple: Fragrant and golden with green, firm leaves on the top.
- Apricots: Slightly soft with a vibrant orange color.
- Cherries: Deep red, shiny, and firm to the touch.

Vegetables:
- Asparagus: Firm stalks with tightly closed tips.
- Peas (snap and snow): Crisp, bright green pods.
- Radishes: Smooth, firm, and brightly colored with fresh, green tops.
- Spinach: Dark green, tender leaves without yellowing or wilting.

Summer (June - August)

Fruits:
- Peaches: Fragrant, slightly soft & golden with a reddish blush.
- Watermelon: "I hope for the best. There's controversy over picking a good watermelon. I think you want heavy for its size with a yellow spot where it rested on the ground. I've always been told that if there's a little drip on the outside by the stem, it sat in the field for a while & should be sweet. But sometimes you never know."
- Blueberries: Deep blue, plump & firm with a silver bloom (a light coating).
- Mangos: Slightly soft & aromatic, with a red, yellow, or green hue depending on the variety.

Vegetables:
- Tomatoes: Fragrant & firm with smooth, shiny skin.
- Zucchini: Small to medium-sized with glossy, blemish-free skin.
- Bell Peppers: Firm, vibrant & heavy for their size.

Fall (September - November)

Fruits:
- Apples: Firm, unbruised & fragrant with a variety of colors depending on the type.
- Pears: Slightly soft near the stem & fragrant.
- Pomegranates: Heavy for their size with deep red, unbroken skin. "We always got these late fall & early winter. Pomegranates were a treat for us & usually something we had at Thanksgiving & Christmas."
- Figs: Plump, soft & slightly wrinkled with rich color.

Vegetables:
- Squash (butternut, acorn): Firm & heavy with matte skin.
- Brussels Sprouts: Tight, firm, bright green sprouts.
- Sweet Potatoes: Smooth skin, free of cuts or bruises.
- Kale: Dark green, crisp leaves without wilting.

Winter (December - February)

Fruits:
- Citrus (oranges, grapefruits, lemons): Heavy for their size with vibrant skin.
- Persimmons: Smooth & bright orange when ripe.
- Kiwi: Slightly soft to the touch with no bruising.
- Cranberries: Bright red & firm.

Vegetables:
- Broccoli: Firm stalks with tightly closed, dark green florets.
- Cauliflower: Firm & compact with creamy white heads.
- Leeks: Firm, straight stalks with white bottoms & fresh, green tops.
- Parsnips: Firm & ivory-colored, similar to carrots.

Tips for Buying Seasonal Produce

- Shop Locally: Farmers' markets often have the freshest seasonal produce.
- Check for Ripeness: Gently press fruits & vegetables to ensure they are ready to eat. I smell them. If you can smell the fruit's "essence" it should be good.
- Avoid Bruising: Select items free of cuts, soft spots, or blemishes or buy them a cut them off.
- Store Properly: Store produce according to its needs (refrigerated or at room temperature) to maintain freshness.

Nourish Your Soul as Well as Your Body

Food isn't just fuel; it's comfort, joy & connection, it's social, it's comfort & care. Never forget the emotional nourishment food can bring, whether through a favorite childhood dish, a comforting bowl of soup when you're unwell, or a warm cup of tea when you're weary.

   -Nani

Vegetable Cooking Time Table

"I learned to boil, steam & roast veggies from my grandmother. If I wasn't sure about something, I looked it up in the cookbook. After that, though, it was just trial & error. I think I burned the peas once by letting the water boil out of them. Be sure to remember to set a timer & to check the water levels when steaming or boiling & to not take your eyes off the broiler. Things can go from great to garbage in an instant. When you're steaming something, remember to take it off the water after it's al dente or fork soft (cooked to your liking) because things continue cooking in the hot water & can become mush. This is when you might want to blanch asparagus, broccoli, cauliflower, cabbage, carrots, Brussels sprouts, beans & peas, to stop them from cooking & keep them bright in color."

-Nani

Tips for Cooking Vegetables

- Roasting: Toss vegetables with oil, salt & seasonings for caramelization & flavor.
- Boiling: Use salted water to enhance flavor & avoid overcooking for vibrant colors.
- Steaming: Retains more nutrients compared to boiling.

Artichokes (whole)
- Boiled: 25-40 minutes (until leaves pull off easily).
- Steamed: 30-40 minutes.
- Roasted: 20-25 minutes at 400°F (200°C) (halved, brushed with oil).

Asparagus
- Boiled: 2-4 minutes (until tender-crisp).
- Steamed: 4-6 minutes.
- Roasted: 10-15 minutes at 400°F (200°C).

Beans, Lima
- Boiled: 8-10 minutes.
- Steamed: 10-12 minutes.
- Roasted: Not commonly roasted.

Beans, String
- Boiled: 4-6 minutes.
- Steamed: 5-7 minutes.
- Roasted: 15-20 minutes at 425°F (220°C).

Beets (young, with skins on)
- Boiled: 20-25 minutes.
- Steamed: 25-30 minutes.
- Roasted: 40-50 minutes at 400°F (200°C) (wrapped in foil)

Beets (old)
- Boiled: 45-60 minutes.
- Steamed: 50-60 minutes.
- Roasted: 50-60 minutes at 400°F (200°C) (wrapped in foil)

Broccoli
- Boiled: 4-5 minutes (florets).
- Steamed: 5-7 minutes.
- Roasted: 20-25 minutes at 400°F (200°C)

Brussels Sprouts
- Boiled: 8-10 minutes (halved).
- Steamed: 8-10 minutes.
- Roasted: 20-25 minutes at 400°F (200°C).

Cabbage
- Boiled: 5-7 minutes (shredded); 10-15 minutes (wedges).
- Steamed: 5-8 minutes.
- Roasted: 25-30 minutes at 425°F (220°C) (cut into wedges or thick slices)

Carrots
- Boiled: 5-8 minutes (sliced).
- Steamed: 5-8 minutes.
- Roasted: 20-25 minutes at 400°F (200°C).

Cauliflower
- Boiled: 5-7 minutes (florets).
- Steamed: 6-8 minutes.
- Roasted: 20-25 minutes at 400°F (200°C)

Celery
- Boiled: 3-5 minutes (sliced).
- Steamed: 5-7 minutes.
- Roasted: 15-20 minutes at 400°F (200°C) (cut into chunks).

Corn (kernels)
- Boiled: 2-3 minutes.
- Steamed: 3-5 minutes.
- Roasted: 15-20 minutes at 400°F (200°C).

Eggplant
- Boiled: Not recommended (absorbs too much water).
- Steamed: 4-6 minutes (cubed).
- Roasted: 25-30 minutes at 400°F (200°C) (sliced or cubed).

Green Beans
- Boiled: 4-5 minutes.
- Steamed: 5-7 minutes.
- Roasted: 15-20 minutes at 425°F (220°C).

Kale
- Boiled: 5 minutes.
- Steamed: 5-7 minutes.
- Roasted: 10-15 minutes at 400°F (200°C) (tossed in oil).

Mushrooms
- Boiled: 4-5 minutes.
- Steamed: 3-5 minutes.
- Roasted: 15-20 minutes at 400°F (200°C).

Onions
- Boiled: 10-15 minutes (whole, small); 5-8 minutes (sliced).
- Steamed: 8-10 minutes.
- Roasted: 25-30 minutes at 400°F (200°C) (halved or quartered).

Peas
- Boiled: 2-3 minutes.
- Steamed: 3-4 minutes.
- Roasted: Not commonly roasted; try 10 minutes at 400°F (200°C) if desired.

Potatoes, White
- Boiled: 10-15 minutes (cubed); 20-25 minutes (whole, small).
- Steamed: 12-15 minutes.
- Roasted: 30-35 minutes at 425°F (220°C) (cubed or wedges).

Pumpkin
- Boiled: 10-15 minutes (cubed).
- Steamed: 10-12 minutes.
- Roasted: 25-30 minutes at 400°F (200°C) (cubed or sliced).

Squash, Acorn
- Boiled: 8-10 minutes (cubed).
- Steamed: 10-12 minutes.
- Roasted: 25-30 minutes at 400°F (200°C) (halved or sliced).

Squash, Butternut
- Boiled: 8-10 minutes (cubed).
- Steamed: 10-12 minutes.
- Roasted: 25-30 minutes at 425°F (220°C) (cubed or sliced)

Tomatoes
- Boiled: Not recommended (can turn mushy).
- Steamed: 3-5 minutes.
- Roasted: 15-20 minutes at 400°F (200°C).

Zucchini
- Boiled: 3-5 minutes (sliced).
- Steamed: 4-6 minutes.
- Roasted: 15-20 minutes at 400°F (200°C).

My favorite memories with my Nani & Popi are:

- Nani's soft & gentle voice
- Cooking Lefsa with Popi
- Being a "farmer" in Nani & Popi's garden & helping them pick fresh vegetables
- Nani & Popi gave me a potted tomato plant & a small notebook with instructions written by Popi on how to take care of my plant. I still have the notebook on my nightstand.

-Paige Avron
(great-granddaughter)

SPICE & HERB SEASONING GUIDE FOR NEW COOKS

Mastering spices & herbs can help transform the simplest of dishes into culinary delights. Always start with a small amount & adjust to your taste. Remember, it's easy to add more but nearly impossible to remove something. This is Nani's guide to growing, picking & using herbs. When in doubt, measure with love.

Herbs: Growing, Picking & Preparing

Growing Herbs:
- Basil: Loves sunlight; water regularly. Grows easily in a garden or a pot. Don't let the leaves get too big, start picking & more will grow. When you harvest it, you can make pesto with it, freeze, dry (by bunching & hanging), remove leaves crush it. Great for pasta & salads.
- Thyme: Thrives in dry soil; perfect for soups & breads.
- Parsley: Easy to grow indoors; garnish for eggs, soups & appetizers.
- Mint: Grows abundantly & is aggressive. When you plant it in the garden, constrain it somehow, or it will grow rapidly & all over. You're better off putting it in a pot; pairs with appetizers & beverages.
- Rosemary: Requires well-drained soil; fantastic for roasted dishes.

Picking Herbs:
- Harvest in the morning for maximum flavor. The juices flow up in the morning & down at night.
- Snip leaves before flowering for the freshest taste. If you start seeing flowers, start snipping.

Preparing Herbs:
- Rinse gently to remove dirt.
- Pat dry & chop finely for even distribution.

How to Use Herbs in Cooking

- Small Amounts First: Start with ¼ to ½ teaspoon dried herbs or 1 teaspoon fresh per serving.
- Timing:
    - Add fresh herbs at the end of cooking to preserve flavor.
    - Add dried herbs earlier to release their essence.
- Pairing Suggestions:
    - Basil: Tomatoes, cheese & eggs.
    - Dill: Fish, yogurt & potatoes.
    - Oregano: Italian dishes, meats & breads.

Seasoning Ideas for Each Dish

Appetizers

- Basil pesto crostini - Fresh basil, garlic & Parmesan.
- Caprese skewers - Basil & balsamic.
- Deviled eggs - Smoked paprika & parsley.
- Garlic herb butter shrimp - Parsley & thyme.
- Mini quiches - Dill & chives.
- Stuffed mushrooms - Oregano & thyme.
- Bruschetta - Basil & garlic.
- Spinach dip - Garlic & parsley.
- Meatballs - Oregano & garlic.
- Cheese crackers - Rosemary & cayenne.
- Roasted chickpeas - Cumin & paprika.
- Caprese salad bites - Basil & balsamic glaze.
- Bacon-wrapped dates - Thyme.
- Guacamole - Cilantro & lime.
- Herbed popcorn - Dill & garlic powder.

Soups

- Tomato basil soup - Basil & oregano.
- Chicken noodle - Thyme & parsley.
- Minestrone - Oregano & rosemary.
- Potato leek - Chives.
- Butternut squash - Sage.
- Lentil soup - Cumin & coriander.
- French onion - Thyme.
- Miso soup - Green onion.
- Clam chowder - Parsley.
- Carrot ginger - Cilantro.
- Black bean - Cumin & chili powder.
- Corn chowder - Paprika & parsley.
- Broccoli cheddar - Nutmeg.
- Split pea - Bay leaf & thyme.
- Tortilla soup - Cilantro & lime.

Breads

- Herb focaccia - Rosemary & thyme.
- Garlic knots - Parsley & garlic.
- Dill bread - Dill & butter.
- Basil tomato bread - Basil & sun-dried tomatoes.
- Cinnamon raisin - Cinnamon & nutmeg.
- Rosemary rolls - Rosemary & olive oil.
- Savory scones - Chives & cheddar.
- Zucchini bread - Cinnamon & nutmeg.
- Sesame breadsticks - Sesame seeds & garlic.
- Onion rye - Caraway seeds.
- Italian herb bread - Oregano & basil.
- Cornbread - Chili powder & cilantro.
- Pita bread - Za'atar.
- Pumpkin bread - Cinnamon & allspice.
- Cheese pull-apart bread - Garlic & parsley.

Pasta

- Basil pesto - Basil, Parmesan & garlic.
- Alfredo - Nutmeg & parsley.
- Marinara - Oregano & thyme.
- Carbonara - Parsley & black pepper.
- Lemon butter shrimp pasta - Dill & parsley.
- Bolognese - Bay leaf & oregano.
- Garlic olive oil pasta - Red pepper flakes & parsley
- Spinach ricotta ravioli - Sage.
- Clam linguine - Parsley & garlic.
- Mushroom stroganoff - Thyme.
- Ziti with marinara - Basil & oregano.
- Cheese tortellini - Basil pesto.
- Primavera - Oregano & parsley.
- Spaghetti aglio e olio - Garlic & parsley.
- Pumpkin ravioli - Sage & nutmeg.

Egg Dishes

- Scrambled eggs - Chives & dill.
- Omelette - Parsley & basil.
- Frittata - Thyme & spinach.
- Poached eggs - Tarragon.
- Deviled eggs - Paprika & chives.
- Shakshuka - Cilantro & paprika.
- Egg salad - Dill & parsley.
- Quiche Lorraine - Thyme.
- Sunny-side-up eggs - Black pepper & parsley.
- Eggs Benedict - Paprika & chives.
- Spanish tortilla - Parsley.
- Egg sandwich - Oregano & basil.
- Hard-boiled eggs - Sea salt & pepper.
- Egg drop soup - Green onions.
- Breakfast burrito - Cilantro & chili powder.

Cheese Dishes

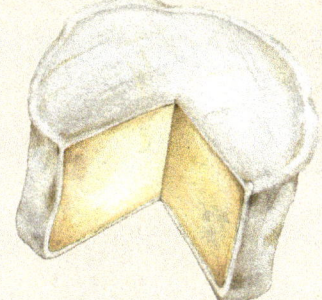

- Mac & cheese - Paprika & thyme.
- Grilled cheese - Basil pesto spread.
- Cheese fondue - Nutmeg & garlic.
- Stuffed bell peppers - Parsley & oregano.
- Cheese soufflé - Chives.
- Cheese scones - Rosemary & black pepper.
- Caprese salad - Basil & balsamic.
- Cheddar biscuits - Dill.
- Cottage cheese dip - Dill & parsley.
- Blue cheese dressing - Chives.
- Ricotta toast - Lemon zest & basil.
- Mozzarella sticks - Oregano.
- Four-cheese pasta - Nutmeg & parsley.
- Baked brie - Thyme & honey.
- Goat cheese salad - Mint & cranberries.

Nani's Key Tips

- **Taste Test**: Add gradually & taste often.
- **Mix Fresh & Dried**: Use dried for depth & fresh for brightness, they just have a lighter flavor.
- **Experiment**: Try a pinch of something unfamiliar to learn its flavor.

As Nani always says," Try, Test & See."

Seasoning is Everything

Just as salt & pepper bring out the flavor of food, small acts of kindness, appreciation & patience bring out the best in life. Season life with love, laughter & understanding.

   -Nani

HOUSEHOLD HINTS

(or hacks as the kids call them)

This is the collection of tricks that Nani learned from her aunt, grandmother, other women & families that shared their tips of the trade, as well as the *Contoocook Cookbook*. As Nani likes to say, "*When it works, it sticks! Collective knowledge passed down can be a beautiful thing.*" We've left space at the end of this section for you to add your own family's tips & tricks.

- After stewing a chicken, let it cool in the broth before cutting into chunks

- For brown crust on roasted chicken, rub mayonnaise generously over the chicken skin before cooking.

- To easily slice meat into thin strips for stroganoff or Chinese dishes, partially freeze it & it'll be much easier to slice.

- A roast with a bone in will cook faster than a boneless roast. The bone carries the heat to the inside of the roast quicker.

- Never cook a roast cold. Let it stand for at least an hour at room temperature. Brush with oil before & during roasting. The oil will seal in juices.

- For a juicier hamburger, add cold water to the beef before grilling. (1/2 a cup to 1 lb of meat).

- Save the juices from your spiced fruits & other canned fruits to pour over ham slices while baking.

- To freeze meatballs, place them on a cookie sheet until frozen in a single layer. Then place in large plastic bags & they will stay separated so that you may remove them as you want

- To freeze berries. Place them on a cookie sheet until frozen in a single layer. Then place in large plastic bags & they will stay separated so that you may remove them as you want.

- To keep cauliflower white while cooking, add a little milk to the water.

- When boiling corn, add sugar to the water instead of salt. Salt will toughen the corn.

- To ripen tomatoes, put them in a brown paper bag in a dark pantry & they will ripen overnight.

- Do not use soda to keep vegetables green, it destroys some of the nutrients, like vitamin C.

- When cooking cabbage, place a small tin cup or can half full of vinegar on the stove near the cabbage. It will absorb the odor. This might work with other odorous dishes as well.

- Potatoes soaked in salt water for 20 minutes before baking will bake more rapidly. "*Just a dash, though, you don't need a lot of salt.*"

- Let raw potatoes stand in cold water for at least half an hour before frying to improve the crispness of French-fried potatoes.

- Use greased muffin tins as molds when baking stuffed green peppers.

- A few drops of lemon juice in the water will whiten boiled potatoes.

- Buy mushrooms before they open, when the stems & caps are attached snugly. This means the mushrooms are truly fresh.

- To cook '*below the ground vegetables*' such as potatoes, carrots, turnips, or beets, place in cold water & bring to a boil. Add '*above the ground*' vegetables like corn, peas, or beans to water that is already boiling.

- Don't despair if you've over-salted the gravy, stir in some instant mashed potatoes & you'll repair the damage in a jiffy. Then, just add a little more liquid to offset the thickening.

- Scissors are a great trick for cutting celery, cucumbers, parsley, mint, lettuce, etc & your kid's food into small pieces. Much quicker & better than using a knife.

- To keep celery crisp & asparagus fresh, stand it up in a pitcher of cold water & refrigerate.

- Lettuce keeps better if you store it in the refrigerator without washing it first, so the leaves are dry. Wash the day you're going to use it. Do not use metal bowls when mixing salad. Use wooden, glass, or China.

- Boil lemon or orange peels to naturally freshen the air in your home.

- Keep one towel for your hands & another for cleaning surfaces to prevent germ spread.

CHEESE GUIDE:
Common & Uncommon

Cheese Name	Appearance	Taste Profile	How to Serve
Cheddar	Firm, yellow or white, smooth surface	Sharp, nutty & tangy	Slice for sandwiches, melt in mac & cheese, or cube for snacks.
Brie	Soft, white rind, creamy interior	Mild, buttery & earthy	Serve with crackers, fresh fruit, or bake with jam in puff pastry.
Gouda	Semi-hard, pale yellow with wax coating	Sweet, creamy & nutty	Slice for sandwiches, pair with smoked meats, or melt into soups.
Parmesan	Hard, golden with a grainy texture	Salty, umami & nutty	Grate over pasta, salads, or soups; eat chunks as a snack with balsamic vinegar.
Mozzarella	Soft, white, smooth	Mild, creamy & fresh	Use in Caprese salads, pizzas, or melt into baked dishes.
Blue Cheese	Crumbly with blue veins	Sharp, tangy & salty	Crumble onto salads, pair with honey & walnuts, or spread on bread.
Feta	White, crumbly, or block form	Tangy, salty & slightly creamy	Sprinkle over salads, mix into Mediterranean dishes, or use in wraps.
Gruyère	Pale yellow, firm with small holes	Nutty & slightly sweet	Melt into fondue, use in quiches, or pair with ham in sandwiches.
Ricotta	Soft, white, slightly grainy	Mild, slightly sweet	Use in lasagna, spread on toast with honey, or mix into desserts like cannoli.
Goat Cheese (Chèvre)	Soft, white, creamy or crumbly	Tangy & earthy	Spread on bread, crumble into salads, or bake with herbs as an appetizer.

Camembert	Soft, white rind, gooey interior	Rich, buttery & slightly tangy	Serve with crusty bread, pair with apples, or bake until melted.
Pecorino Romano	Hard, pale yellow, grainy	Salty & sharp	Grate over pasta, mix into pesto, or shave onto salads.
Provolone	Semi-hard, pale yellow, smooth	Mild to sharp (aged varieties)	Slice for sandwiches, melt into casseroles, or cube for antipasti platters.
Havarti	Semi-soft, creamy with tiny holes	Buttery, sweet & mild	Slice for sandwiches, pair with figs, or melt into grilled cheese.
Halloumi	Firm, white, smooth	Salty & slightly tangy	Grill or pan-fry for salads or serve as a stand-alone appetizer.
Manchego	Semi-hard, ivory-yellow with wax rind	Buttery, nutty & slightly tangy	Serve with olives, slice for charcuterie boards, or pair with quince paste.
Cotija	Hard, crumbly, white	Salty & tangy	Crumble onto tacos, soups, or corn on the cob.
Paneer	Soft, white, firm texture	Mild & slightly milky	Use in Indian dishes like curries or grill for salads & wraps.
Burrata	Soft, white ball with creamy center	Rich, creamy & buttery	Serve fresh with tomatoes, olive oil & basil; or use as a pizza topping.
Fontina	Semi-soft, pale yellow with tiny holes	Buttery, nutty & slightly tangy	Melt into pasta dishes, use in fondue, or slice for sandwiches.
Raclette	Semi-hard, pale yellow with firm rind	Creamy, nutty & slightly fruity	Melt over potatoes, bread, or vegetables in traditional raclette dishes.

Taleggio	Semi-soft, pale orange rind, creamy	Tangy, fruity & slightly earthy	Melt into risottos, serve with crusty bread, or pair with pears.
Comté	Firm, pale yellow with smooth texture	Nutty, buttery & slightly sweet	Slice for cheese boards, melt into gratins, or pair with white wine.
Asiago	Hard or semi-soft, pale yellow	Mild to sharp (depending on aging)	Grate over pasta, use in salads, or slice for sandwiches.
Queso Fresco	Soft, white, crumbly	Mild & slightly tangy	Crumble onto tacos, soups, or salads; use in Mexican dishes.
Stilton	Firm, blue veins throughout	Bold, tangy & creamy	Crumble into salads, pair with figs, or serve with port wine.
Mascarpone	Soft, creamy, white	Mild, buttery & slightly sweet	Use in desserts like tiramisu or spread on toast with honey.
Caciocavallo	Firm, golden rind, teardrop shape	Mild & tangy	Slice for antipasti platters, grate over pasta, or serve with prosciutto.
Appenzeller	Semi-hard, pale yellow, firm texture	Spicy, nutty & aromatic	Serve with bread, melt into fondue, or enjoy with fruit.
Epoisses	Soft, orange rind, creamy center	Rich, pungent & tangy	Serve with crusty bread & a robust red wine.

Cooking is a Gesture of Care

Making a meal is more than just feeding someone, it's a way to show them we care. This lesson reminds us that our actions, especially the small ones can be expressions of love.

-Nani

NANI'S RECIPES FOR LIFE

It's common knowledge within our family that Nani has the best advice, not only when it comes to crafting the perfect sauce or cookie recipe, but concerning the big things in life as well. The insights & 'Life Recipes' included here have been copied from text messages received by Nani, in her own words.

While Nani has never claimed to be a doctor or medical professional & we as a family are in no way dispensing medical advice, these brilliant notes have definitely helped to ease the things that have ailed us & we're confident that they'll bring a little bit of peace & joy to your life as well. As Nani always says, 'when it comes to matters of chocolate & love, measure with your heart.'

- For Worry:

Worry does nothing to fix or solve our problems. Instead, try praying for mental peace. When all else fails, put your feet up & have a cup of tea with your favorite gal.

- For Anxiety:

Anxiety requires too much physical action & energy but deep breathing & exercise can often help deliver peace & ease. Prioritize having time for yourself everyday as a means of prevention, not just as a reaction.

- For Fulfillment:

Remain grateful for of all your blessings everyday *(even the little ones)*, it brings great fulfillment if & when you're able to see things that way. Sometimes it helps to keep a little notebook handy, to write 3 things you're grateful for each day.

- For a Long Marriage:

Consistent communication, flexibility, patience & care in all ways & situations. Always remember, you are a team & stronger together.

- *For Tough Conversations:*

Rely on honesty & not accusations. Sometimes, silence is required more than words.

- *For Having MORE Fun:*

Make time to prioritize your mental health. Put it on your schedule so it becomes reality & remember, a little spontaneity won't hurt your responsibilities.

- *For Taking Care of Responsibilities:*

Never put off what must be done. Pay your bills on time. Keep your word. Ask for help from others if needed. When you find yourself needing help to better your work or to find work, pray to St. Joseph, *the patron saint of workers,* for support & guidance.

- *For Overcoming Fears:*

Face them head on & pray the for strength needed to overcome them.

- *For Finding Lost Items:*

Back track your last steps & try to picture the last time you had them. If all else fails, sit quietly & pray to St. Anthony for guidance.

- *For Creating Prosperity:*

Try to put a little something away from each paycheck. Be frugal. Learn the difference between wants & needs. Educate yourself to gain skills, build confidence in yourself & strengthen your ability to communicate.

- *For Health:*

Get outside, eat more nutritious foods than anything else, exercise & keep moving. Have fun & enjoy the life you have created. Keep a positive attitude. You can also pray to St. Raphael the Archangel for healing, especially regarding physical ailments.

DEAR NANI:
A letter to our beloved matriarch

Dear Nani,

As I sit in your kitchen, my arms resting on the familiar green & wooden countertops, I find myself trying my best to transform the overwhelming emotions I feel into words. While this love note comes at the end of your cookbook, what I'm writing isn't a conclusion. I'm setting out to write a celebration of a woman who possesses the deepest & most profound love, creativity, joy, loyalty & generosity.

There really are no words grand enough to capture what you mean to this family. *If there were, however, they would surely be written in sauce-stained ink, passed down in the form of handwritten recipes & served at a table where there's always room for one more.* You've fed our family in every way possible; mind, body & soul. From your schnitzel to your legendary spaghetti sauce & Thanksgiving feasts to the simplest gouda grilled cheese sandwiches that somehow taste so much better when you make them. Your hands have never just prepared meals; they have created memories. Each & every dish you craft carries with it the love, patience & pride that only you could pour into those moments.

When we think about you, Nani, it's impossible not to giggle about the iconic way you purse your lips or stick out your tongue when focusing on something particularly intricate & are totally in the zone. Whether you're hammering schnitzel, peeling apples for a pie, or sewing, this is a Nani trait that's so simple & yet so you; endearing, funny & completely characteristic of the thoughtfulness & care you put into everything you do. These little quirks of yours always make us smile & represent so much more than just food. They represent your attention to detail, your patience & your dedication to making sure every dish you prepare is just right & presented with care. Your kitchen is where your love flourishes & we are the lucky recipients of that love.

From your hands to ours, you've made sure that these recipes will continue to nourish us, both physically & emotionally, for countless years & generations to come. Your innate understanding of what we need, what we love & what will make us feel special is a testament to how deeply you know & cherish every single member of your family.

Your grandchildren gush about the deep sense of love & connection that always fills them up when they're with you. It's those simple, joyous times when the family gathers around your kitchen table, spilling over with laughter & conversation. These are the memories that keep us grounded, reminding us of what's really important in life. We are all especially fond of your famous schnitzel, a dish that's become a signature family meal. As we continue your tradition of passing this recipe down to our own families, we can only hope to do it justice & prepare it with the same love & care you've always shown. You've taught us not just to cook but to connect, to fill our homes with love & laughter & to pass on the things that matter most.

But your gifts extend far beyond the kitchen. You & Popi have built a home that feels like a warm embrace, where every person, whether born into this family or lucky enough to marry in, knows they are deeply loved. The echoes of laughter around your table, the quiet moments of grace before a meal, the way conversations linger long after plates are cleared, these are the things that make our family whole.

We've watched as you've cared for each of us in the smallest but most meaningful ways. Whether it's making sure each person gets their favorite meal, knowing exactly where the hidden bean dip would be, or placing pillows on the bench so the little ones can reach the table, your love is in the details. And, even when you try to stay out of the kitchen, we all know you can't help but hover; watching, guiding & of course offering your expert advice when needed. You, Nani, are the heart of this family. You fill us up, not just with your incredible food, but with your unwavering love, your wisdom & the traditions you've built over a lifetime. Because of you, we know that family is more than just the people we are born to—it's the people we sit beside, share meals with & cherish, no matter how far away from each other life takes us.

I am humbled to have played a small part in telling this story. I've had the deepest cries here, at this familiar counter, some tough conversations & insurmountable laughs where my belly ached from pure joy. This kitchen has held it all for me. Every moment spent here feels like a brushstroke in a masterpiece of memories.

I've had the profound honor of compiling this cookbook for you. Your once-upon-a-time wish for each of your family members has become a treasure trove of love. And, as I embraced the journey, I did my best to allow these pages to unfold as a work in progress. By far the most meaningful part was getting to connect with each family member as they, too, shared their personal memories, their laughter, their gratitude & their favorite moments spent with you.

As tears stream down my face, once again & I look at these pages, I know there are no words to express the gratitude & appreciation we all have for you & Popi, the extraordinary couple that started it all. The two of you brought each one of us into this world & we are so joyfully stitched together by your bond.

I say there are no words & yet I wish I could write forever about the life you've given us. I've had 37 years of the greatest love I've ever known. 37 years of hellos & phone calls I never want to end. 37 years of birthday cards with stickers, hugs that linger & "I love yous" that fill your cup when you need it most. I think of Uncle Chip, your firstborn, who's had 62 years (& counting) of loving you. And I think of the miracle that first brought you & Popi together so many years ago.

As the countless special memories came flooding in from the family, your family, it brought me such joy to see the little things that each of us values. Each of us remembers something a little different in our own ways, but also share something so similar, being seen, heard, appreciated & deeply loved. That is the truest testament to your unwavering love.

Your home is a sanctuary, a place where love is served in abundance. Your philosophy has always been simple, meals nourish both the body & the soul. Food has been your way of bringing people together, celebrating, comforting & sharing joy. There are no secrets in our kitchen, just like love is meant to be given & received, so are our recipes & values.

You taught me how to cook by doing. Hands-on, side by side, with laughter & stories, passed down as we stirred sauces & rolled dough. I now pass on that tradition to my own daughter, knowing that with each meal we make together, we continue your legacy of love.

So with this book, the collection of your recipes & a handful of our memories, we want to say thank you. For every meal, every hug, every moment of grace. For the way you make each of us feel seen & special. For the love that fills every corner of your home & every heart in this family & beyond.

With all our love,

Your Family

(written by Jessica Greenlow)

TO MY FAMILY

A Note From Nani

To my Family,

I get my joy for cooking from my MeMe (Cornelia Merkelbach Breault). She was a master in the Kitchen, preparing Gastronomical feasts for a family of 10.

Today, cooking for my family is my greatest joy. Gathering around the table, sharing our traditions from Lupe to Lasagna brings me comfort + pride.

It is such a pleasure sharing recipes and preparing them with my children (all great cooks in their own right) and just being with them all together at family dinners, holiday gatherings, tea parties and celebrating great grand childs birthday dinners — warms my soul.

I feel blessed to share my joy of cooking with our family and hope they feel comfort in knowing they will never go without.

There will always be a place for them at Nexi's table.

Love Nexi

FULL INDEX OF RECIPES

A

B

Bacon Wrapped Asparagus - 105
Baked Beans - 142
Baked Ham - 202
Balsamic Rosemary Carrots - 36
Banana Bread - 215
BBQ Hamburgers - 140
Better Than Robert Redford - 222
Blackberry Muffins - 218
Bread Dressing (Stuffing) - 22
Breakfast Egg Bake - 92
Brunch Quiche - 122
Butter Balls (aka Italian Wedding Cakes) - 53
Butter Toffee with Nuts - 66

C

Canadian Oatmeal Shortbread - 156
Charcuterie Board - 96
Cheesy Garlic Bread - 106
Chewy Almond Cookies - 64
Chewy Molasses Cookies - 154
Chocolate Crinkles - 84
Coleslaw - 143
Corned Beef, Cabbage & Potatoes - 112
Cranberry Relish - 23
Crêpes - 120
Crock Pot Bean Soup - 184
Crustella - 56
Cucumber Sandwiches - 152

D

Date Filled Cookies - 48

Dill Pickles - 177

E

F

Fattigmanns Bakkels - 74

Fermented Sauerkraut - 114

Filled Molasses Cookies - 60

Fresh Fruit Salad - 136

G

Gingerbread Babies - 62

Gnocchi - 172

Goulasch - 182

Grammie Lupo's Giamboto - 169

Grampie Lupo's Spaghetti Meat Sauce - 163

Grandma Avron's Potato Lefse - 40

Grandma Avron's Prune Dressing - 21

Greek Salad - 137

Green Beans with Bacon - 24

Green Beans with Garlic - 44

Green Peas with Bacon - 43

Grilled Chicken Breasts - 134

Grilled Steak Skewers - 132

Guinness Beef Stew - 116

H

Haddock Au Gratin - 209

Hazelnut Cake - 220

Homemade Pesto - 170

Honey Garlic Glazed Carrots - 27

I, J

K

Krumkake - 91

Kvikke Brod (Norwegian Flatbread) - 71

L

Lentil Soup - 190

Low Sodium Cream of Celery Soup - 192

Low Sodium Cream of Chicken Soup - 191

M

Macaroni & Cheese - 196

Mary's Instant Potato Lefse - 203

Mashed Potatoes - 26

Mashed Sweet Potatoes - 206

Mexican Pinwheels - 197

Minestrone Soup - 188

N

Nani's Famous Lasagna - 100

Nani's Meatballs - 168

Nick's Favorite Tuna Casserole - 200

O

Open-Faced Salmon Finger Sandwiches - 150

Oven Baked Fish - 210

P

Pan Seared Salmon - 211

Pasta Salad - 144

Peanut Butter Cookies - 72

Peanut Butter Fudge - 68

Pecan Pie - 108

P continued

Pecan Tarts - 65
Pistachio Biscotti - 58
Pizza Cheese Fondue - 80
Pizzelles - 55
Popi's Favorite Apple Pie - 30
Pork Chops - 204
Pork Schnitzel - 34
Potato Salad - 146
Pumpkin Pie - 28

Q

Quick & Easy Sauerkraut - 113

R

Roast Beast & Gravy - 98
Roasted Brussels Sprouts - 104
Roasted Turkey & Gravy - 18
Rumtopf - 76

S

Salmon Patties - 208
Seafood Chowder - 194
Scalloped Potatoes - 102
Shepherd's Pie - 198
Snickerdoodles - 214
Spaetzle - 173
Spanakopita - 124
Split Pea Soup - 193
Spritz Cookies - 70
Stromboli - 174
Sugar Cookies with Frosting - 50

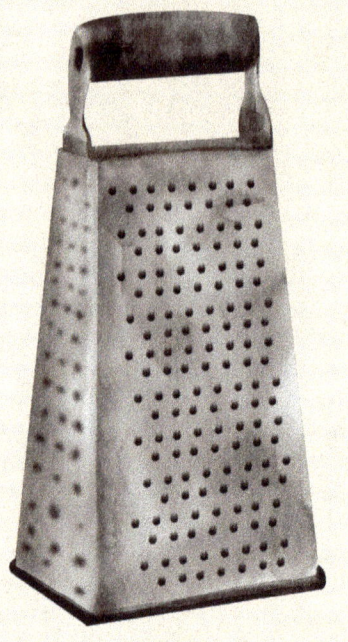

S continued

- Swedish Coffee Ring - 88
- Sweet Cornbread - 212
- Sweet Potatoes - 25
- Sweet Ricotta Pie - 126
- Swiss Cheese Fondue - 82

T

- Tenderizing Brine - 178
- Tortellini Soup - 181
- Turkey & Stuffing Meatloaf - 180
- Turkey Chili - 186

U

V

- Venison Meatballs with Brown Gravy - 38
- Viking Coffee - 224

W, X, Y

Z

- Zucchini Bread - 216

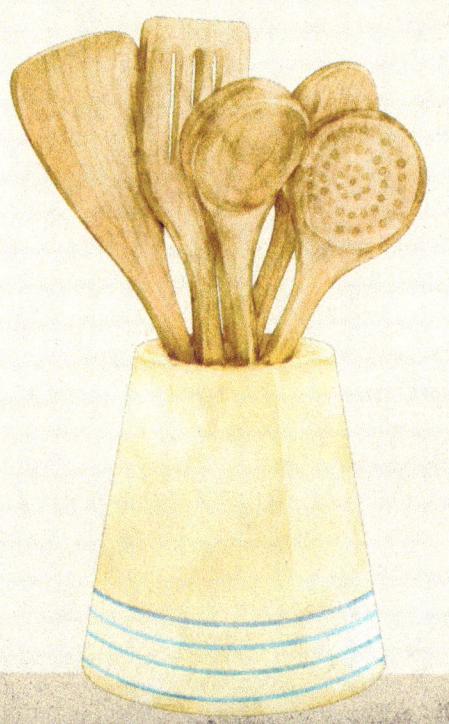

www.ingramcontent.com/pod-product-compliance
Lightning Source LLC
Chambersburg PA
CBHW061401010526
44107CB00012B/1015